Signs for These Times

Church Signs that Work

Ronald T. Glusenkamp

CPH
SAINT LOUIS

To my wife, Sue Ann, and our three children, Nathan Theodore, Noah Timothy, and Hannah Grace, for they have truly been signs of God's love and grace to me.

> There is a time for everything, and a season for every
>   activity under heaven:
> a time to be born and a time to die,
> a time to plant and a time to uproot,
> a time to kill and a time to heal,
> a time to tear down and a time to build,
> a time to weep and a time to laugh,
> a time to mourn and a time to dance,
> a time to scatter stones and a time to gather them,
> a time to embrace and a time to refrain,
> a time to search and a time to give up,
> a time to keep and a time to throw away,
> a time to tear and a time to mend,
> a time to be silent and a time to speak,
> a time to love and a time to hate,
> a time for war and a time for peace *(Ecclesiastes 3:1–8)*.

Jesus did many other miraculous signs in the presence of His disciples, which are not recorded in this book. But these things are written that you may believe that Jesus is the Christ, the Son of God, and that by believing you may have life in His name *(John 20:30–31)*.

CONTENTS

ACKNOWLEDGMENTS

A book is the work of many people. I graciously give thanks to God for my parents, Levera and Frank Glusenkamp who first shared with me the story of Jesus and His love. I am grateful to the dedicated people at Concordia Publishing House, especially Barry Bobb, Ruth Geisler, Rachel Hoyer, and Dawn Weinstock. I would like to thank James Heine from Editorial Solutions for his guidance and gracious suggestions. I give thanks for the helpful insights from Carol and Tripp Frohlichstein of MediaMasters. I am indebted to Jerry Berger of the *St. Louis Post-Dispatch* for his SIG-Nificant assistance in getting the word out. Last, but not least, I give thanks to God for the members, staff, and friends of Gethsemane Lutheran Church, St. Louis for their prayers and partnership in the ministry of Jesus Christ.

Prologue

There is the story of a sign above the doors to a church that reads in bold, beautiful script, "The Gates of Heaven." Beneath the doors on a piece of cardboard is handwritten in crayon, "Please use side entrance." I don't know if this particular story is true or not, but I am certain that mixed messages like this are sent out by people of good will. Faithful people who want to invite other people to church sometimes end up sending contradictory signals. Imagine, if you will, another faux sign (based on a blooper) that reads,

---

DON'T LET WORRY
KILL YOU
LET THE CHURCH HELP!

Obviously, the writer of the message wanted to encourage people to de-stress their lives. However, the sign is distressing because it implies that church could help kill you. In fact, the church proclaims the message of Jesus, who said, "I have come that they may have life, and have it to the full" (John 10:10).

This book is about how your church sign can be a 24-hour evangelism tool, and you will have the time of your life doing it. It will help you realize and maximize the potential of your sign. By following the advice and principles articulated in this book you will be able to present a clear, focused message that enlightens and entertains people who drive and walk by your church. For example,

---

IN LIFE'S OLYMPICS,
GO FOR THE GOLD ...
IN KINDNESS

Another sign that sets the tone for what I am talking about:

SUNDAY'S SERMON TOPIC:
"WHAT IS HELL?"
COME EARLY & LISTEN TO OUR CHOIR!

I suspect whoever composed such a sign would not receive a very harmonious reception by the music staff. They would probably direct the author of the sign to take note and say something more appropriate!

How much better to have a message that would help people tune into the Good News of Jesus Christ. What could be better than to state the following?

WE'RE OPEN EASTER SUNDAY
BECAUSE THE TOMB
WAS OPEN EASTER SUNDAY!

Or something along the line of

EVERY SUNDAY HERE
IS
SUPER SUNDAY!

This book will help you connect with people by creating signs for these times. It will describe the conversation that can be struck up with people who pass the church every day. You will be able to create a dialogue with people hungry and thirsty for the Good News. Because the signs are current, relevant, and biblically based, you will be able to help people in their faith journey.

The following signs offer invitations. The first one has its basis in a promotion by a fast-food restaurant. The other is linked to the arrival of a new software product.

**READ THE BIBLE
& GET YOUR FAITH
SUPERSIZED—FOR FREE!**

**OUR WINDOWS
WILL HELP YOU
UPGRADE!**

It is as the psalmist invited, "Taste and see that the Lord is good" (Psalm 34:8).

How We Became the Church with the Sign

> I love to tell the story of unseen things above,
> Of Jesus and His glory, of Jesus and His love
> I love to tell the story, because I know its true;
> It satisfies my longings as nothing else would do.
> I love to tell the story, I'll sing this theme in glory
> And tell the old, old story of Jesus and His love.

I love to tell the story of Jesus and His love. I have found that a church sign is one of the best ways to communicate the story of Jesus and His love. Inspiration for the sign came from Habakkuk 2:2 when God told the prophet to "Write down the revelation and make it plain on tablets, so that a herald may run with it."

Your congregation probably has a sign in front of its building. (If it doesn't, how do visitors know who you are?) Most likely, the potential of this sign is not being maximized. What's even worse, it might be communicating something negative about God and/or your community of faith (more on this later).

This book is intended to inspire, explain, and be a resource of how a routine aspect of a church property can become an extraordinary, 24-hour-per-day witness to the Gospel and a point of great interaction with the community around the church. Your sign can be an evangelism tool for getting your congregation known in the community and connecting faith life with daily happenings. It can be a way to connect with "some [who] have never heard the message of salvation from God's own holy Word," and "for those who know it best, seem hungering and thirsting to hear it like the rest" (verses 2 and 3, *I Love to Tell the Story*).

People are thirsty for the refreshing Good News of Jesus Christ. However, sometimes individuals and congregations are guilty of the criticism leveled by one contemporary author that we promote thirst without quenching it. What an indictment! It ought to move us so that we spring into action to meet the needs of those who hunger and thirst for the Living Water.

The encounter at the well that Jesus had with the Samaritan woman can be a model and a challenge for the outreach of your sign. He told her, "Everyone who drinks this water will be thirsty again, but whoever drinks the water I give him will never thirst. Indeed, the water I give him will become in him a spring of water welling up to eternal life" (John 4:13–14).

Your church sign can be an oasis for people experiencing a very dry time in their lives. It can give them a sip of what your congregation is all about. Better yet, it can help them experience the refreshing and renewing Water of Life, Jesus Christ.

Whenever I tell people in our community where I am the pastor, their response is, "Oh, you're the church with the sign!" My immediate response is a big smile as I say, "Yes, we are." Not long after I arrived at Gethsemane Lutheran Church, someone asked, "What do you think you want on the marquee?" *Marquee*— the word struck me because it didn't sound very church oriented. I almost corrected the questioner because his choice of words sounded too much like show business to me. But the more I thought about it, I realized a marquee is exactly what a church sign can be.

The dictionary defines marquee as (1) a large tent with open sides, used chiefly for outdoor entertainment; (2) a rooflike structure, often bearing a signboard, projecting over an entrance, as to a theater or hotel; (3) a star performer, someone or something people go out of their way to see.

I like the idea of having a big tent—it sounds very biblical to me. However, we don't have a tent, only a sign used primarily to convey information in a humorous manner. So instead of listing only the times of services and the name of the preacher (which members should already know) and interested parties can find by calling the church's voice mail, perusing its website, or walking through the yellow pages, we decided to have some fun with the sign. I know from the comments I receive in person and through the mail that the sign provides "outdoor entertainment," and is the opening for coming back to church or attending for the first time. Some people tell me they go out of their way just to drive by the church to see what's on the sign. Several people who have visited Gethsemane told me they come to our church because they thought any church that has a sign like that is something they wanted to be a part of.

Our church building is located at the corner of a busy intersection with a stop light. People are headed in all four directions. As folks drive by or stop at the light, the sign gives them a moment to reflect. At any given time, people are experiencing problems at home or with a promotion at work; there are losses to be accounted for and gains to be celebrated. The sayings on the sign are directed at people going through these experiences. As Ecclesiastes states: "There is a time for everything, and a season for every activity under heaven" (3:1).

It is my hope and prayer that people going through good or bad times in their lives will be touched by the joy the sign reflects. I want people to drive by (or walk or jog or ride by) and at first laugh or chuckle, but then think about what the sign is saying. Just because the mission of the church making Christ known is serious business doesn't mean we can't project joy and peace. Our sign generates conversation. It makes our members proud of their church and provides an opportunity to share the Gospel. Many of our members tell me that their neighbors and friends comment or ask about the quotes on the signs.

Our church sign is a popular topic of conversation in other areas as well. One saying on the sign was in the *National Enquirer* (see Roseanne Barr), another was in *The American Banker* (see the

Boatman's Guy), *The Orange County Register*, and some of the sign sayings are frequently mentioned in the *St. Louis Post-Dispatch*, *The St. Louis Lutheran*, and *Southside Journal*. The sign has also been part of TV stories regarding mission projects of the congregation, and it is often commented on by radio talk show hosts. It is important to note that while we are known as "the church with the sign" we are not "the sign with the church."

It is my prayer that your church can become "the church with the sign" as you proclaim the Gospel through the words you put on your sign.

Ron Glusenkamp

Practical Stuff

Jesus said, "For God so loved the world that He gave His one and only Son, that whoever believes in Him shall not perish but have eternal life" (John 3:16).

At the beginning of each worship service, I make the sign of the cross and say, "In the name of the Father, and of the Son, and of the Holy Spirit." For several years I have told each confirmation class that the cross is the best *designer* label, for it bears the name and mark of the Holy One who calls us through the waters of Holy Baptism to be His daughters and sons. The cross is the sign for all seasons. It reminds us of who we are and whose we are.

As we go about our lives, as we meet each other on the cross walks of life, as we sometimes say cross words to each other, as we participate in double crosses or are betrayed by a double cross, as we find ourselves entering or exiting a crossroad in our careers or personal lives, it is as St. Paul wrote, "for the message of the cross is foolishness to those who are perishing, but to us who are being saved it is the power of God" (1 Corinthians 1:18).

The church sign stands in the shadow of the cross and the empty tomb. It is on the other side of Easter. Because Jesus died on the cross and rose from the dead, we have a wonderful message to share with the world.

WHAT'S YOUR SIGN?

The question, "What's your sign?" has more to do with the placement and visibility of your church sign. Normally, the most effective placement of the church sign is perpendicular to the street. This placement gives the traffic passing on both sides of the street an opportunity to see it. I have seen church signs parallel to the street. Sometimes that placement is for aesthetic considerations, but it isn't the most effective use of the sign. The visibility of the sign is decreased, offering a smaller window of time to view it.

Think about the people driving by your church, and consider where your sign can make the best impressions. To revise a popular advertisement, "This sign's for you!" The church sign is not really for the members, but for prospective members and friends of the church. If the sign is too close to the building, it will simply blend in with the background. If your church sits on a boulevard you might want to place the sign at an angle to the building. Consult with local zoning officials for any codes regarding the use or size limitations of signs. (I have found employees of the sign company most helpful in giving expert advice on the placement of your sign. They are the experts in aiding churches and businesses.) Stand at various angles and look at the proposed placement of the sign. Are there other signs across the street or in the background that might overshadow your sign? Signs attached to chainlink fences don't seem appropriate. Furthermore, they may make a more negative statement when there is nothing on the sign!

Most church signs can be illuminated. A simple rule of thumb is to let your light shine 24 hours per day. The church is all about letting our lights shine. Why have a sign that's not illuminated at night? It has been my experience that people driving by churches at that time really need a message that enlightens and entertains. The cost savings in terms of electricity are inSIGNificant when compared to the opportunities. People need to perceive the church as a place where the light of Christ is reflected. If other signs in your neighborhood are off at night, just imagine how your sign can stand out during these particular times.

I have seen the following message on several churches and think it is effective:

——

IF YOU ARE LOOKING
FOR A SIGN FROM GOD
THIS IS IT!

——

WHOSE SIGN IS IT?

Many churches assign different committees to oversee various aspects of congregational life. While it is very important to have committees that function, sometimes they don't work the way they need to. I remember a wise person once saying to me, "Look at the statues in the parks, not a one of them is in honor of a committee. Rather, they are in honor of one person." Having said that, I must also say that committees have their place and role in the life of congregations. Two of the most important committees in any church are the Evangelism Committee and the Property Committee. Sometimes, though, these committees are at cross purposes. The Evangelism Committee wants to have the doors wide open for everyone. The Property Committee remembers the last time the doors were wide open. The floors got dirty, walls had to be repainted, and the cooling bill was out of control. The Property Committee wants the facility to look as good as it possibly can. They would love to have the Evangelism Committee recruit new members who would sign up to participate in the Property Committee's annual "Tuck Pointing and Gutter Cleaning Extravaganza." The Evangelism Committee wants the church to look good because it will be more attractive to prospective members who may join the Evangelism Committee. The Evangelism Committee is chaired by someone who is like Mary, who wants to sit at the feet of Jesus and learn more about living and loving. The Property Committee is chaired by someone like Martha, who believes one can learn more about living and loving through scraping chewing gum off the bottoms of pews.

Usually, the church sign is the domain of the Property Committee. While this might be a good idea if electrical wiring needs to be run out to the sign, it can be rather shocking what kinds of messages the Property Committee wants on the sign. Conversely, I don't know that I would have the Evangelism Committee in charge of the wiring. Instead of infusing the church with Spirit, fuses might get blown.

Instead of being at cross purposes, both committees—in fact, all committees—should remember the purpose is to proclaim the wonderful message of the cross. "For the message of the cross is foolishness to those who are perishing, but to us who are being saved it is the power of God" (1 Corinthians 1:18).

WHEN YOU'VE INHERITED A BAD SIGN

A popular saying from a few years ago, "What you see, is what you get," holds true for church signs. Unfortunately, you may not like what you are getting from your church sign. After reading this book, you may have discerned that your church sign is one of the following:

- It is a stealth sign. When people are asked how they liked this week's sign message, their response is, "What sign?"
- It has only been repainted once after it was first used as a door of a Castle Church in Wittenberg during the 16th century when someone nailed 95 statements on it.
- It follows the biblical principle, "Now we see but a poor reflection as in a mirror" (1 Corinthians 13:12). The glass is broken and the letters are illegible.
- Neighboring churches beg you not to change your church sign because it makes their church sign look good.
- Family members donated it in memory of a matriarch or patriarch of the congregation. Unfortunately, the brass plaque listing the names of the donors is larger than the name of the church on the sign and twice as valuable as the sign.
- All of the above.

My advice when you've inherited a bad sign is to do your homework. Research the influence or lack of influence the church sign is having. Ask members and friends of the congregation these questions:

1. What does the church sign say about who we are?

2. What does the church sign say about whose we are?

3. If you were driving by today, what would you think about the church sign?

   You'll be amazed at what people say.

So you have done your homework, researched the sign's influence, and you are excited—you want to get a new church sign. An appearance before the Property Committee has been arranged. You walk in, confident of your cause, but just two minutes into your presentation someone interrupts you. I know from being involved with churches all my life that this person will say, "I don't think our sign is so bad. Besides, it costs money to change to a new sign." Those two sentences contain three issues that have dominated church meetings for centuries:

1. "Low self-esteem" regarding types of materials and resources churches should use

2. Money

3. Change

I suggest the best way to answer these objections is to respond by stating the cost that could be incurred because people are not attending the church. Maybe the church's public face (including the church sign) doesn't look inviting. If the goal is to share the message of Jesus Christ, why wouldn't a church want to do its best to accomplish that goal? The cost of a new church signs varies, but they can run between $4,000 and $7,000. If you calculate it, the cost is about $20 per day for a year. Make a challenge to congregation members to sponsor a "day" for the new sign. Birthdays, anniversaries, and graduations could be sponsored for less than a dollar per hour. Donors will be enthused that their gift will help the church share its message with more people. If your congregation has a memorial fund, perhaps that money could be used to finance the sign. Or ask the pastor if someone has offered to make a donation for something special. The church sign can be that special something that promotes all that happens at church.

Furthermore, maybe the sign "isn't so bad," but ask the question, "Is it so good?" Ask the committee to think of restaurants and businesses they frequent. Do their signs make a good presentation, or do they appear to be saying, "If you don't have anything better to do, come on in."

Enthuse the Evangelism or Outreach Committee with your vision. They may have been struggling with the question of how to make the church better known in the community. The Social Action Committee can also assist by having the church sign support public service announcements. Budget constraints and limitations these days are real. However, they need not end your quest for a new church sign. You're bound to run into some detours or bumpy roads along the way, but keep in mind that Jesus is the Way, the Truth, and the Life (John 14:6).

BASICS

If you are in the market for a church sign, visit with the representatives from local sign companies. There are two basic types of signs, single face and double face. Normally, it isn't good to be "double faced," but I suggest you make an exception when it comes to selecting a church sign. A single face sign is appropriate if traffic is coming from one direction only. A double-face sign gives you many more options (two different messages at the same time) with a higher rate of making impressions.

The most popular size of church signs is 4' × 8'. It can either be set up with a "post" mount, which is normally included in the base price, or it can have a "base mount," which may include a pedestal of brick or stone work. This is an extra item that can be provided by volunteers from the church or contracted through the sign company.

The letters of the alphabet are routinely 4" or 6". I think the bigger the letter, the more striking and bold the image is. Letters are usually black, but some suppliers carry red, blue, and green. You might want to experiment with different colors during various seasons of the church year, or use simple, black letters. Try to make your words and messages as colorful as can be. For example, one of our denomination's college jazz bands was on a tour and was scheduled to play at our church. St. Louis also has a hockey team called the Blues and they were going through a slump, so the following sign was inviting:

GOT THE BLUES
FREE JAZZ CONCERT!
7 P.M. SATURDAY

When the church sign is used to reflect the promises of God's love and grace, you can be assured it will brighten people's days.

....

The Sign Changer

When people ask me who changes the sign week after week, year after year, I always tell them that I have been blessed with a wonderful member, Don Sandberg. Don has been the "signmeister" for almost a decade. He receives assistance from Rollie Walston and Hub Frederickson (both of them promised me if I put their names in this book they would always agree to change the sign, even during bad weather!). It is very important to have someone besides me put the messages on the sign for several reasons. First, four eyes are better than two eyes. By adding another person to the process, you sharpen your focus and prevent mistakes and offenses. Don feels very comfortable asking me to rethink a word or two in a message. Sometimes we have disagreed whether anyone will understand a particular sign. At times these discussions are simply the result of our being from two different generations, which brings up an interesting point. Not everyone will understand or appreciate every sign. I remember once when we were putting up the *karaoke* sign. Don had his trusty dictionary and couldn't find the word in it. At the same time, there were three local establishments that had it in big bold letters. We ended up putting it on the sign:

BETTER THAN KARAOKE,
COME SING WITH US

On occasion, the sign message will not work due to space or letter limitations. I know several pastors who write the messages and change the signs too. It is a reality that many times the pastor also types the bulletin. I believe this is a ministry that should be shared. Conversely, I don't think an individual or group of people should put things on the sign without the minister reviewing it. Follow these simple rules when planning your sign:

- AsSIGN someone to do the sign.

- CoSIGN the messages; in other words, do them together.

- DeSIGN a place that isn't visual pollution. Don't put a cardboard sign or other signs next to your church sign. Too many signs detract from the main church sign.

- Re-SIGN or change the sign frequently. A good rule of thumb is that a sign probably has a life of a week to 10 days. Even the funniest signs get old. If it's really a good sign, you can bring it back in a year or two for an encore performance.

A Short History of Time
and the Church Year

Having a church sign is really about stewardship, utilizing a gift that has been given. The outdoor sign at our church was here when I came. It had the usual boring information on it—times of service, minister's name, and identification of the denomination. From time to time the sign was changed, but there wasn't a plan or even an appreciation of the effect we could have with the sign. In fact, it didn't really enter much into the thinking of our evangelism program at all. Then one day, all that changed when I did a sign about Roseanne Barr. It was right after she "sang" the national anthem. It was fall, when many congregations recruit choir members, so I put up the following sign:

<hr>

ROSEANNE BARR DOESN'T
SING HERE,
BUT YOU CAN!

<hr>

Many people took note, and the response was a chorus of positive comments. It was written up in the *St. Louis Post-Dispatch*. Someone even took a picture of it, sent it in to *The National Enquir-*

er, where it was printed in color. Little by little, people were talking about the sign; not just members, but folks who drove by the church. They would call the secretary or tell me they went out of their way to see what was on the sign. I secretly wished my sermons were that popular. I suppose they would be if I limited content to six or eight words. Anyway, the more feedback I received, the more I thought about the sign as a way to enlighten and entertain many people.

It is estimated the average person receives about 16,000 messages each day. That is a lot of information to process. How many of those messages enlighten and entertain? The answer, unfortunately, is very few. People will remember the messages that bring a smile to their face or make them think.

Noted hymn writer Rev. Jaroslav J. Vajda wrote a hymn that addressed the cacophony of sights and sounds that bombard us every day. The first verse says it well.

> Through the din of life around me
> Comes a haunting song of love.
> One can hear it glowing, growing
> Like a rainbow through the clouds,
> Made in heaven, full of promise,
> Bringing peace and joy and comfort,
> Let me learn that song of praise—and sing along.

Now, the only din I knew was Gunga Din. But din is the onslaught of all the messages that beep, ring, buzz, and vibrate in our lives. It includes the e-mail and the junk mail, the snail mail and the express mail. This din is the 16,000 messages that come to us daily. Included in all of it are signs. As the Five Man Electrical Band lamented, "Sign, sign, everywhere a sign!"

Through the din of life around me, comes a haunting song of love. The Bible is, among other things, a collection, an anthology if you will, of love songs. They describe a God who creates, redeems, and renews us again and again through love while reporting the ups and downs of the people of God. There are love songs about the birth of visions and the death of dreams, the lonely times walking in the valley of the shadow of death, and the joyful times of reunions and homecomings.

It is interesting to note all the times singing takes place in the Bible. After a great act of salvation, people gather like Moses, Aaron, and Miriam (the first family musical trio) to sing. During times of sadness and grief, the children of Israel sat by the waters of Babylon and sang the blues. Angels sang at the birth of Christ, "Glory to God in the highest and peace to God's people on earth." Conversely, at times of sickness and death, plaintive, haunting laments are echoed and repeated, "Woe is me. Why is this happening?" The early church gathered together and was refreshed by "psalms, hymns and spiritual songs" (Ephesians 5:19). Sometimes the song we hear is the consensus of a group. It proclaims what we have been unable to say or pray as individuals.

I think of Christmas Eve when I hear " Silent Night." I don't know whose house is silent, calm, and bright on Christmas Eve, but that song takes us to a place that is. At other times, a song such as "Amazing Grace" directs our thinking and praying as individuals. These oldies but goodies are on the hard drives of our hearts and brains. They take us back to places and times we remember as calmer and simpler. And the Bible also calls us to sing a new song (Psalm 96:1) and to make a joyful noise (Psalm 66:1).

A well-tuned church sign can be seen and "heard" despite the din of life. When your church sign sings the *haunting song of love*, others will be drawn to sing along with you. Like the positive message sign of the rainbow, people will smile and remember God's promises when they read the sign.

CHRONOS AND KAIROS

When the Bible mentions the word "time" more than fourteen words are used. However, they don't all mean the same thing. For example, there are two Greek words, *kairos* and *chronos*, which both mean time, but different aspects of it. *Kairos* is the right time, a period of opportunity, a season. *Chronos* is a measurement of time; it is a fixed point in time.

"After John was put in prison, Jesus went into Galilee, proclaiming the good news of God, 'The time has come' He said. 'The

kingdom of God is near. Repent and believe the good news!' "
(Mark 1:14). The word for time in this passage is *kairos*. The time in
Ecclesiastes 3 is also *kairos*. In other words, there are seasons of time
that flow into each other. *Chronos* is the word used for time in the
following passage, "Then Herod called the Magi secretly and found
out from them the exact time the star had appeared" (Matthew 2:7).

I have found that people whose internal clock runs on *kairos*
often marry someone whose clock runs on *chronos*. My wife, Sue
Ann, is a wonderful, caring, loving, and giving person. She is also
kairos oriented. I like to think of myself as having the same char-
acteristics as Sue Ann, but I am *chronos* driven. When a person
calls the church and asks, "What time are your services?" I don't
respond by asking, "What time can you get here?" Rather, I say,
"They are at 8:30 and 11:00 A.M."

If Sue Ann and I have a noon lunch date, it is my understanding that noon is twelve o'clock sharp. Sue Ann's understanding of noon is anywhere from 11:30 A.M. until 2:00 P.M. Her
window of "noon" is opened much wider than my 60-second
interval of noon. Added to this situation is the reality that the spiritual life of most people runs on *kairos* time as they go through the
seasons of life. Unfortunately, the church approaches people more
from a *chronos* or chronological perspective, as if all 20-year-olds
and 65-year-olds are the same.

The church sign should have some *chronos* information on it—
the times of services and other special events. However, it really
needs to have its internal clock set on *kairos*. Think of it this way—
the church sign can be a "Son-dial" for people who don't have
enough time. The sign can connect with them during these times
and help them come to the knowledge that Jesus is "the Alpha and
the Omega, the Beginning and the End" (Revelation 21:6).

———

ARE YOU WEAKENED
AFTER THE WEEKEND?
GET RE-CHARGED WITH GOD!

———

WANT SPICE IN YOUR LIFE?
SPEND THYME AT CHURCH
AND BECOME A SAGE!
ROSEMARY DID!

TIME

I was waiting for the light to change at the intersection and looked at the vacant building in front of me. The clock that once graced it is no longer there. I read someplace it was taken down for repairs. I thought to myself that the barren storefront clock was an accurate diagnosis of many people living in a "time-oriented" society. Even though we have all these time-saving devices, we don't seem to have enough time or even know what time it is. Jesus said, "Therefore keep watch, because you do not know the day or the hour" (Matthew 25:13). I was deep in thought when horns started honking behind me. I guess the driver right behind me was trying to indicate what time it was. But it made me recall an experience I'm sure you've probably had. It is the day after Halloween and the candy is marked way down, the colors of orange and black are gone. There are little elves, candy canes, reindeer, snowflakes, and the latest animated animals or dinosaurs singing a medley of "Joy To the World," "Jingle Bells," and a reggae version of "Silent Night." Christmas by most calendars is still nearly eight weeks away, but it appears it will occur that very night.

Just one day after Valentine's Day, a local store in my neighborhood had all its Valentine candy on sale. As I looked at the table of discount candy, my eyes were drawn to the main candy aisle (similar to the valley of the shadow of death). The space that just two days before had been filled with chocolate hearts was now the coop for marshmallow chicks, the burrow for chocolate Easter bunnies, and a plethora of jellybeans. Easter Sunday was at least two months away, but now was the time to stock up on plastic green grass and egg-dyeing kits.

The same store started selling Christmas ornaments in July (for those who want to beat the Labor Day rush) and often has Halloween items mixed with the "back to school" specials. One friend of mine is constantly ahead of the game; her family celebrates Christmas at Thanksgiving, New Year at Christmas, and so on. Therein lies the dilemma, for in the commercialization of the incarnation of our Lord and His miraculous birth in Bethlehem, many people lose sight of the "reason for the season." Connected to that issue is the reality that Jesus may come again tonight or tomorrow. And that possibility is so pregnant with possibilities for you and me and for our world that we don't know exactly what to do.

We are overwhelmed and, like the folks who Paul was writing to in Thessalonica, there are a couple ways to respond. Some folks felt the return of Jesus was so imminent (like next week) there wasn't any point in doing anything. Why do homework, rake the leaves, rehab houses for the homeless, if our Lord is returning soon? At times these people are so obsessed with the imminent return, they can't think of anything or even anyone else. They ignore the pain and suffering around them because all will be gone in the life to come. At the other end of the spectrum is the attitude of the happy hedonist, who doesn't see purpose except for the moment. Live for today, weekends were made for beverages brewed in St. Louis. You only go around once in life, so reach for the gusto. Another aspect of not knowing what time it is results in being so consumed in the moment that you forget the past and can't think of the future.

Have you ever been at a child's basketball or soccer game or school play and been trampled by overanxious videographers? My own children believe we are the only family in the universe without a video camera. But if you ask one of the camera operators if they saw a certain thing, their usual response is, "No, I was too busy taping to see what was happening. But I 'm going to watch the tape when I have time." It is important to look to the future and to record the present, but I think by putting a majority of our lives on "fast forward," we miss important events happening today.

A friend of mine told me he was confronted by a participant in a 12-step program who said to him, "You have been so caught up in your career that you've been a 'human doing' not a human being!" My friend said that those words at that particular time in his life really spoke to him. He is now working on living like a "human being" and taking life one day at a time. An equal problem rests with living in the past. I used to cringe when my parents or grandparents would say, "In the olden days ..." Now I find myself saying things like that to my children or to the confirmation class all the time.

So how do we make or take time? The church year is a wonderful resource in helping us know what time it is. It is also a fabulous way to mark the days of our lives, so they have meaning and purpose and are filled with what God is calling us to do. "Jesus Christ is the same, yesterday, today, and tomorrow" (Hebrews 13:8). In this time-oriented society, we have instant coffee, fast foods, same-day surgery, quick copies, one-hour photo labs, and minute-by-minute updates on radio and television. To answer the questions: Does anyone know what time it is? Does anyone care? The church answers yes and yes. Yes, we know what time it is, namely God's time. And yes, we care, and so does God! It is helpful to ask, "What time is it?" That was a popular question on the minds of the disciples. They wanted to know when all the wonderful things Jesus had spoken of would come into fullness. In addition, they wanted to help rush the plan. But, Jesus said, "The right time for Me has not yet come" (John 7:6).

As we draw closer to the end of this century, thoughts and questions about time will become more and more prominent in daily discussions. In trying to help people understand time, I often say, "Picture, if you will, God holding a slinky in His hands. God is the beginning and the ending, holding time before Him. As an old gospel hymn states, "We don't know what the future holds, but we know who holds the future."

The prophet Isaiah proclaimed the Word of the Lord, "For My thoughts are not your thoughts, neither are your ways, My ways," (Isaiah 55:8). I am at the same time comforted and put into place by that statement. God's ways and times are different than ours. Peter wrote, "But do not forget this one thing, dear friends: With the Lord a day is like a thousand years, and a thousand years are like a day" (2 Peter 3:8). The key point to remember during these times is to be "with the Lord." For when we are "with the Lord," we begin to understand that God's timetable is in His hands, just as the whole wide world is, too.

Whose time is it? The abbreviation A.D., short for the Latin *Anno Domini* means "in the year of our Lord." This particular designation has pretty much been dropped from everyday terms. However, it is still "in the year of our Lord." Imagine how each day might begin with a new sense of purpose and meaning when it is begun with that acknowledgement in mind, "Today is God's time."

We have two weekends a year when we "spring forward or fall back." The hands of the clock are moved ahead one hour in the spring, and they are moved back an hour in the fall. The time change in the spring makes everyone "lose" an hour. This phenomena inspired me to put up a sign:

DID YOU LOSE AN HOUR?
FIND THE TIME OF YOUR LIFE
AT CHURCH!

---

and

LOSE AN HOUR?
SO DID PASTOR.
SHORT SERMON ON SUNDAY!

Consequently, the time change in the fall prompted the following sign:

USE YOUR EXTRA HOUR
TO MAKE ST. LOUIS BETTER!

TIME BYTES

Digital watches enable us to keep track of smaller bytes of time. Our days and nights are split and divided into all sorts of pieces of time. There is lead-time and just in time. There are part-time and full-time jobs. We anxiously await game time and hit the refrigerator during half time; there is prime time on television and certainly time bombs (some of the TV programs themselves). There is party time and nap time. There are time shares at resorts and opportunities to share time with family and friends. There are time capsules buried in the ground, and time release capsules in our medicine cabinets. There is time-lapsed photography and lapses in time when we forget appointments.

How we perceive time depends on many variables. I remember a Bible class when a retired person lovingly said to a young mother, "You know, you are always asking the question of how to be good or do good. And at this time in my life, I am thinking about how good it is going to be." This woman was in a different season of her life than the young mother. She was thinking about eternal life whereas the young mother was thinking about how to live her life because of what the Eternal One has done for us.

People who are or were raised on farms have a different experience about time than people who live in urban areas. Country people know that when it is harvest time, there is an imperative sense of it all. Conversely, people whose time is apportioned out into microseconds get frustrated when they have to wait a minute or two.

I remember the punchline of a joke that had the pilot of an airplane telling the passengers, "I have good news and bad news. The bad news is, we are lost. The good news is we are making very good time!" On Super Bowl Sunday 1998, networks charged $3,000,000 per minute for advertising. This rate transferred over to the length of the sermon that Sunday as a $37.5 million bargain.

These are very good times to convey messages that enlighten and entertain people who might be lost. These are very good times to help your community take time to contemplate God's timetable. A wonderful hymn, "Crown Him With Many Crowns" reminds us we are called to:

> Crown Him the Lord of years,
> The potentate of time,
> Creator of the rolling spheres,
> Ineffably sublime.
> All hail, Redeemer, hail!
> For Thou has died for me;
> Thy praise and glory shall not fail
> Throughout eternity.

Your sign can help people know what time and whose time it is. Consequently, they will have more times of peace in their lives.

PASTOR'S SERMONS ARE SHORT,
BUT "SHORT" IS RELATIVE WHEN
YOU ARE TALKING ABOUT ETERNITY!

AN ALTERNATIVE LIFESTYLE

The church year follows the life, death, and resurrection of Jesus Christ. It begins with the season of Advent and concludes with Christ the King Sunday. While the church year was for many years and for many people the "clock" by which their world was organized, it is in these times an alternative lifestyle. For example, Pentecost Sunday came and went without taking anyone's breath away. I wasn't invited to any Pentecost Parties. (I think that's because there weren't any.) Nobody sent me a Pentecost card. I stopped by the mall and didn't notice any Pentecost Weekend

Sales. The sports channels weren't filled with Pentecost Bowl games. Traffic was light because there weren't any Pentecost Parades. Here is the birthday of the church, yet no sign of a cake with almost 2,000 candles on it (talk about *Waiting to Exhale!*). And yet, Pentecost is such an inspiring day. For people who suffer from communication breakdowns, Pentecost is the ultimate communication breakthrough. The church year sets a rhythm to help us walk through and make sense of these times.

A few years ago around Reformation Sunday, I received a phone call from a woman representing an organization that helped needy children. She told me about an event that was taking place the last Sunday in October. When I told her our congregation was supportive of the cause but wouldn't be able to participate because we were already committed to a citywide Reformation Day service, there was silence. And then she said, "Reverend, you are the third Lutheran pastor I've talked to today who told me about the Reformation Day Service. Do you Lutherans always schedule Reformation Day Service around Halloween?" My response was, "No, Halloween is always scheduled around Reformation Day." The sign that came out of that conversation was,

---

IT'S A TREAT,
NOT A TRICK!
GOD LOVES YOU!

It is important to know your audience. What connection can you make with what is happening in the world and what is happening because of the Word, Jesus Christ? While most of North America gets caught up in the weather prognostications of a Ground Hog on February 2nd, the church year calendar observes this day as the Presentation of Christ. A great way to make the connection between shadows is to connect it to the Light! Consequently, a sign could read,

---

SEEING SHADOWS?
COME TO THE LIGHT!

Or do some kind of play with the words, "weather" and "whether:"

———

WHETHER OR NOT IT'S SHADOWS
CHURCH CAN HELP YOU
WEATHER THE STORMS OF LIFE!

———

WE BELIEVE THAT SOMEONE ELSE
KNOWS MORE THAN THE SHADOW KNOWS!

———

The only downside of a one-day event is you have to change the sign as soon as it out of date. Go through the church calendar and see how the calendars of school, sports, and community events overlap. Sports follow a cycle of sorts. The opening day of baseball is always perceived as a new beginning when hope springs eternal. Some seasons overlap, such as hockey, baseball, and basketball, all taking place at the same time. The academic season or calendar is of interest if you live in a community that is really focused on the beginning of school, holiday breaks, finals, and graduation. A few years ago, a sign on a church by a university read:

———

WE WILL HELP YOU STUDY
FOR YOUR FINAL EXAM

———

Hunting season is important in many communities. It resonates with a great many people. While the tensions around hunting are significant, it could be worth a sign, welcoming hunters and reminding them there is no limit on kindness. I don't really know enough about it to say more, except to remind folks:

———

OUR OFFERINGS SUPPORT MISSIONS
AROUND THE WORLD, SO
THE BUCK DOESN'T STOP HERE!

———

Warning—this sign may not *en-deer* you to everyone. They just might not *fawn* over it. But, *doe-n't* let that worry you.

Paul wrote, "Do not conform any longer to the pattern of this world, but be transformed by the renewing of your mind. Then you will be able to test and approve what God's will is—His good, pleasing and perfect will" (Romans 12:2). The church sign is a fantastic way to help people "walk the talk" and remember significant events in the life of Christ and the church. Use it to enlighten people to this exciting alternative lifestyle.

TIME, THE CHURCH, AND YOUR SIGN

I remember an older pastor telling me he didn't mind when people looked at their watches during the sermon. It was when they took them off and shook them to see if they were still working that troubled him. Time and church are an interesting combination. If a movie or dramatic presentation at a theater lasted 59 minutes, it is quite possible you would feel shortchanged. However, if worship lasts longer than 60 minutes, some people get concerned and agitated. A professional baseball game or football game would hardly be completed in just 60 minutes. So I find it curious that in most aspects of our life, we want more but, when it comes to church, we believe less is more.

Given the time constraints of busy lives, I don't know how to resolve the tensions involved with time and church. However, I believe time spent in church, worshiping God and hearing the Word, celebrating communion, and praying for yourself and others is the most important way we can spend time. The church sign is a 24-hour invitation and reminder to people to "take five," whether that five is allotments of seconds, minutes, hours, days, weeks, or years.

Many churches encourage tithing. Most often it is only associated with gifts of money. What if we thought about tithing time? There are 168 hours in a week. If we tithed the week that would be 16.8 hours. Even if one was to subtract 56 hours for sleep (something I think we'd all love to have), 102 hours remain to use as a base for tithing time. And even if you subtract 50 of those hours for work/school requirements, 52 hours could be used as a base for tithing.

I can't promise you that a witty, creative church sign will automatically mean people will want to spend more time in God's service, but I can promise you that the church sign can and does make an impact on the lives of folks who read it. Isn't it about time to turn the tables on time?

SOME DOS AND DON'TS

Dos

Just writing the word *do* makes me think about the words that used to be called homonyms but are now frequently called homophones. The word *do* also sounds like two other words, *dew* and *due*. Nike sportswear exhorts people to "Just Do It." So does James, "In the same way, faith by itself, if it is not accompanied by action, is dead" (2:17).

When God responded to the grumbling of the children of Israel (Exodus 16:13), maybe He said, "Just Dew It." Manna was, after all, a dew-like substance. And what about what is due unto others? "Give to Caesar what is Caesar's and to God what is God's" (Matthew 22:21).

Words like *alter* and *altar* are frequently misspelled in church bulletins. I've seen bulletin announcements for the "Alter Guild." Now, granted the altar guild is responsible for a lot of changes—alterations, if you will—but the connection between that and the piece of furniture at the front of most sanctuaries can really help people alter their life.

DO YOU WANT TO ALTER YOUR LIFE?
WE STILL MAKE ALTAR CALLS!

LOOKING TO ALTER YOUR LIFE?
COME TO THE ALTAR OF LIFE!

Or you could take a popular phrase like "no man is an island," and make it a little more of an inclusive, contemporary statement:

NO ONE IS AN ISLE
FIND COMMUNITY
IN ONE OF OUR AISLES!

One of my favorite word plays came to mind a few Easters ago, when I was buying dye for our Easter eggs. With all the emphasis on the Easter Bunny, candy, and baskets, this was the message:

EASTER IS MORE
THAN SOMETHING
TO DYE FOR

The word play here is simply "egg-shellent!" The two words being connected are *dye* and *die*. The saying also picks up on a common phrase that something is "to die for." Using the homophone *dye* for the word *die*, adds color to the discussion about the centrality and importance of the Resurrection.

Another Easter sign picks up on a song from the 1970's and deals with the issue of grief:

MOURNING HAS BROKEN
ON EASTER MORNING!

Wisdom is always needed when playing with two words that sound alike. For example, *bridle* and *bridal*. While Scriptures talk about not being unevenly yoked (2 Corinthians 6:14), I don't know if I'd try to horse around with a sign connecting those two. There is the connection to *getting hitched*. However, proceed with caution unless you want someone to *nag* you about this *bit*. It could *stirrup* too much trouble and *saddle* you with controversy. Someone might try to *rein* you in, even *shoe* you the road.

Obviously, the point is to have fun with words. Just spend a few moments making the connection between words that sound alike. Two words that come to mind are *acts* and *ax*. Those two words don't seem to have much in common, except for a critic who has reviewed a drama and done a *hatchet* job on it. However, if you think about acts in a drama and brainstorm a few moments about *ax*, John the Baptist comes to mind. He played a significant role in announcing the coming of the Lord. He is also seen as one who *cuts through* all sorts of things. So maybe an eye-catching sign would read:

**JOIN US FOR THE READING OF
THE AX OF JOHN THE BAPTIST.
STUDY THE ACTS & ROOTS OF CHRISTMAS!**

It may not be a home run, but it might help you get to first base with someone. A sign of note that might strike a chord with some readers is:

**OUR AREA HAS
LOTS OF ARIAS
COME SING WITH US!**

**WE TRUST IN BALMS
NOT BOMBS!**

A helpful exercise is to just have some fun with the following combinations of words. Many of them have some church connection. Write them down and make your own sayings with them.

arc and ark

baa and bah

cannon and canon

cents and scents and sense

censer and censor

chance and chants

———

SINCE THE 13TH CENTURY
OUR CHANTS
LEAVE NOTHING TO CHANCE

———

air and heir

idle and idol and idyll

incite and insight

knave and nave

knight and night

knead and kneed and need

missals and missiles

morals and morels (morels are an edible fungus)

profit and prophet

A sign could read:

———

WE DIG MORALS & MORELS
WE HELP FAITH
MUSHROOM & GROW!

———

CHURCH IS A HEALTHY PLACE.
WE PASS THE PAX,
NOT THE POX

———

A local car wash usually displays the following sign during spring:

———

**THE WEATHER SERVICE IS
A NON-PROPHET ORGANIZATION**

———

I recently was at a playground and the sign at the entrance of the play area read:

———

**NO RUNNING
NO SHOUTING
NO SAND THROWING
NO FOOD OR DRINK IN AREA
NO JUMPING
HAVE A NICE DAY!**

———

Dos

The purpose of the church sign is to help people have a nice day. Here are some *dos* I have learned while paying the *dues* and also getting some *dew* on my shoes when I've had to change the sign.

1. Do have fun.
2. Do take chances.
3. Do watch TV and listen to the radio to hear the latest catchy slogans and phrases.
4. Do read the newspaper and the Bible.
5. Do be respectful of your congregation's and community's culture.
6. Do listen to what people are saying or not saying about the sign.
7. Do change the sign on a weekly basis.
8. Do build up and don't tear down.
9. Do ask, "Does this sign enlighten and entertain?"

Don'ts

1. Do not take yourself too seriously (these are signs, not commandments).

2. Do not worry when you get a negative comment. (Someone suggested every negative comment should be reprogrammed and count as four unspoken compliments.)

An effective church sign resembles a conversation between good friends. The language and tone of the discourse is based on mutual respect and admiration. The tone of the conversation is casual; it doesn't shout, scream, yell, or holler. Ultimatums or threats don't have a place in such a dialogue. As a Christian who dearly loves the church, it pains me to say I am often deeply offended by some of the sayings I read on church signs. The offense is not based on the scandal of the crucified Christ (1 Corinthians 1:22–23), but is generated from an unkind spirit. In other words, the sign comes from meanness or haughtiness. In some ways it comes across as, "We have it and you don't, too bad!" A popular sign on church lawns is:

—

NO JESUS—NO PEACE
KNOW JESUS—KNOW PEACE!

—

While Christians believe and teach that because of Jesus there is a "peace of God that transcends all understanding" (Philippians 4:7), my feeling is that sign sayings like that and the one that follows are descriptive in nature and don't have enough to include a prognosis. Church signs should be about a joyful *insight*, not a woeful call to *incite*. The purpose is to share God's peace and not tear someone to pieces. A sign I often see during the season of Lent reads:

—

IF CHRISTIANITY WERE A CRIME,
WOULD THERE BE ENOUGH EVIDENCE
TO CONVICT YOU?

—

Obviously, the intention of the sign is to make a person feel guilty that he or she hasn't committed enough "crimes" to warrant an arrest. My hunch is the person who doesn't know Jesus Christ as Lord and Savior will not understand the subtle nuances of the saying. He might simply plead, "No Contest." It is quite likely those who do know Jesus Christ as Lord and Savior will either feel cross that a particular church is judging them or feel sadness about their own faith journey.

It has been my experience that the signs that really connect to people reflect a sense of humor and a feeling of empathy. Isaiah was called by God to, "Comfort, comfort, My people, says your God. Speak tenderly to Jerusalem, and proclaim to her that her hard service has been completed, that her sin has been paid for, that she has received from the LORD's hand double for all her sins" (Isaiah 40:1–2).

In a world that is at times very uncomfortable and inhospitable to people who attempt to walk in the footsteps of our Lord and Savior Jesus Christ, how significant it is to be a place that promotes God's soothing words of comfort and warm words of welcome.

I see lots of signs that don't reflect the joy of the Gospel. They seem rather legalistic, negative, and judgmental. Words like *should*, *ought*, and *must* regularly appear along with serious realities like *sin*, *death*, and *hell*. At times the rhetoric on these signs has an "insider" quality. You would have to be well versed in that particular denomination's history and use of language to understand it. On the other hand, don't be shy about stating quite boldly "who we are and whose we are." The church sign is different than the sign for the local bank or service station. It is appropriate and even commanded that Christians let their light shine before others, "that they may see your good deeds and praise your Father in heaven" (Matthew 5:16).

Another way to think of it is that a church sign is like a snapshot. Our immediate reaction is, "That's not how I look, is it?" Your church sign is a little snapshot of who and what your church believes about God, how it feels about major issues of the day, and what its sense is about the times in which we live. It is a challenging task to say something faithful, humorous, and inviting in a few brief words. And yet, that's part of the fun.

Here are some suggestions to consider when creating sayings for the sign, along the lines of the sign being a "snapshot" of your congregation's faith journey:

- Make sure there is plenty of light and lite in the picture.
- Focus on the positives.
- Direct attention to the Word.
- Flash—make it timely.
- Expose the values and benefits of being loved by God.
- Try it from a couple of different angles.
- Leave it to the tabloids or someone else to develop the negatives!

CHURCH SIGNS FOR "DUMMIES"

A good friend of mine suggested that I call this book "Church Signs for Dummies." While the thought of capitalizing on the trend of many authors to write for beginners or novices initially appealed to me, it would be contrary to the theme of this book: to help people create signs that enlighten and entertain. It would be an insult to others at the same time. However, that is exactly the impression many church signs convey. I can only guess what is the thought or (lack of thought) and motivation behind some of these signs.

I remember learning the phrase, "Sticks and stones may break my bones, but words will never hurt me." Nothing could be farther from the truth. Words are powerful. They can tear down or build someone up. Successful church signs are in the construction business. It is much better to build up than to tear down.

Martin Luther wrote about this in his explanation to the eighth commandment, "What does this mean? We should fear and love God so that we do not tell lies about our neighbor, betray him, slander him, or hurt his reputation, but defend him, speak well of him and explain everything in the kindest way." I have found from personal experience that the eighth commandment is one of the most difficult to follow. I am saddened to say at times I have been the sender and at other times the receiver of words and messages that were not the most loving or kind. This is not a new problem. James clearly states, "With the tongue we praise our Lord and Father, and with it we curse men who have been made in God's likeness. Out of the same mouth come praise and curses" (3:9).

The proliferation of shows like "Hard Copy" and "A Current Affair" gives plenty of testimony that there is a seemingly endless market for half-truths, innuendoes, and unconfirmed reports. And yet, people of God are called to be above that type of talk and behavior. In addition, we are called to defend and befriend our neighbors when untrue things are said or written about them. The church sign can be a tool to fight hate speech in your community. The sign can offer insight when other media only present messages that incite.

The following sign lifted up the illuminating aspects of three community holiday festivals, Advent, Hanukkah and Kwanza:

**CELEBRATE THE LIGHT AND WARMTH
OF ADVENT, HANUKKAH, AND KWANZA.
LET YOUR LIGHT SHINE!**

TONE OR CHARACTER

A question I often ask people who want to know about the tone or character of the sign is, "Would you rather receive a summons or an invitation?" A summons is often delivered by an officer of the court and is an important document. However, it's also associated with legal proceedings and affairs of a court. An invitation is usually associated with a celebration of some kind—birthday, anniversary, or graduation. A summons demands time and appearance, whereas an invitation leaves the decision open to the recipient of the invitation. Even when a congregation thinks it is being inviting, it can be issuing a summons.

For example, many churches have made the decision to be more welcoming to guests and visitors. They put the following saying on their sign, "Visitors Expected." It might be better if the sign read, "Visitors Anticipated."

This is a wonderful time to ask who is the intended audience of the sign. If it is visitors or guests, then I think the wording should be more invitational. If it is the members and staff of the congregation, then the sense of expectation could be conveyed through means not so public.

....

HUMOR

One of the major goals for the church sign is to provide an opportunity to have a time to laugh. Laughter is being recognized more and more as providing a significant role in well-being and even healing. Medical researchers encourage us to laugh, indicating laughter has benefits, such as producing endorphins that act to reduce stress and pain and generate feelings of good will. Norman Cousins often called laughter, "inner jogging." (And if I'm going to do any kind of jogging, it's going to be inner and not outer.)

We often laugh when we experience or see something we did not expect. Laughter is a way to respond to change. Sarah laughed when she was told she and Abraham would be parents. When the long-awaited child was finally born, he was called Isaac, which means laughter. Sarah and Abraham, along with God, shared in the joy of that wonderful event. The psalmist knew, "Weeping may remain for a night, but rejoicing comes in the morning" (Psalm 30:5).

Due to the space limitations of a church sign, much of the humor revolves around word play or puns. Humor is serious business. Note the increase in comedy clubs around the country. Comedians provide insight on the social scene while tickling our funny bones. And yet, humor is also something that should be handled with care. Jokes and remarks that tear down others are totally inappropriate. Churches are perceived as places of welcome and sanctuary. In a world that at times seems to be very inhospitable, a church sign can provide of humorous word of welcome. For example, in 1997 while scientists were finding signs of life on Mars, the following sign graced our front lawn:

MARTIANS WELCOME!
WE HAVE SPACE
FOR EVERYONE.

I also know from personal experience that sometimes the desire to play the clown, to be the top banana is not always *a-peeling*. Sometimes it ends up making me look like a monkey and ultimately detracts from the message I want to communicate. In fact, instead of drawing a *bunch* of people into a church community, this desire to be the *top banana* only makes them want to *split*. (See I told you, sometimes you ought to stop sooner.)

Furthermore, one needs to be cognizant of what topics or areas of life can be addressed in a humorous manner and also by whom and in what setting. Any kind of tragedy or catastrophe is totally out of bounds for an attempt at humor. While the hosts of late-night talk shows might be able to gain laughs at the political foibles and peccadilloes of politicians, I have found it is best to stay away from those topics.

The signs I come up with tend to go more for a chuckle than for a response of shock. During the spring of 1998, a new medicine, Viagra (which is prescribed to treat impotency in males) received a great deal of attention. The public was well aware of this new product. Even a former senator who was the Republican presidential candidate in 1996 said he had participated in the protocol study of Viagra. So, it was a popular topic. Now, at first blush it would seem that a sign incorporating the name of this new product would be appropriate, so I wrote:

THE SERMONS HERE ARE
MORE UPLIFTING
THAN VIAGRA!

Obviously, this particular sign elicits a chuckle, but we must realize some topics are not appropriate for church signs. I would not put that particular saying on our sign. It probably would be considered offensive and in poor taste and might even shock some people. But just because we would not go for shock doesn't mean that a John-the-Baptist-type of message to the community is inappropriate, and it can be a niche for your particular sign.

This is a debatable topic. A local pastor whom I respect very much is a good sign writer. The Rev. Jeff Long, pastor at Zion United Methodist Church, was a journalist before he became an ordained minister. He knows how to use a headline to grab attention. He has said, "There is so much clutter, so many things to look at that you have to cut through all that clutter. I want to be funny and invitational. I don't want to be *cute*. I'd rather have people stop and think. If I have to make a choice between being cute or being shocking, I'd rather do shock!"

When I asked Rev. Long to share some of his favorite signs with me, he chose the following:

MIKE TYSON,
GOD WILL LEND YOU
HIS EAR!

CARDS OVER YANKS IN 6
JESUS OVER DEATH IN 3!

GOD IS ALWAYS ONLINE
NEVER A BUSY SIGNAL!

COME TO CHURCH.
RESISTANCE IS FUTILE.
YOU WILL BE ASSIMILATED.
WE'RE NOT BORGS—WE'RE METHODISTS.

—

DON'T HALE BOPP
HAIL CHRIST
HE GIVES LIFE—DOESN'T TAKE IT.

—

When asked to describe his approach, Rev. Long states, " In a cocooning kind of a world, where you can't really go door to door any more, the sign becomes an opportunity to reach people. I want people to think maybe there is something at that church for them."

As I think about some of those signs Rev. Long shared with me, I have mixed feelings. First, I admire his ability to take a very current situation and make a short comment on it. Second, I appreciate his courage. I am sure he received mail or phone messages not particularly supportive of his humor (quite possibly they were from some of his own members). And third, it really comes down to what one wants to do with the sign. And some of that has to do with where the sign is located.

The sign at Zion United Methodist Church is on a very busy road. There is not a stop light or stop sign nearby, so the signs really have to catch the driver's eye. Rev. Long is utilizing his sign to draw people's attention to it for a moment or two. Consequently, shock or something very much out of the ordinary is the name of the game for that sign. Rev. Long realizes his background in Top 40 radio might make some of his audience switch stations, so he usually checks a new saying by running it by someone he trusts. This type of collaboration is appropriate and important.

I am sure that some people felt the Mike Tyson sign was tasteless (pun intended). Others would be offended by the fact that sports and the Resurrection were linked together. Yet, at the same time, I am certain there were people who said to themselves, "Wow, that church really knows what's going on." These reality bytes are intended to connect with people not presently connected to church. Therefore, I like what Rev. Long does because it is consistent with who he is and what his vision is for his congregation.

I try to follow St. Paul's words about building up. "Do not let any unwholesome talk come out of your mouths, but only what is helpful for building others up according to their needs, that it may benefit those who listen"(Ephesians 4:29). For example, it is one thing for me to make a joke about Lutherans to other Lutherans (because I am one) in an informal setting such as Bible class or study group. But I don't know that I would put a joke on the church sign. And when a person of another denomination makes a joke about Lutherans, I may not think his or her remarks are so funny. Part of me wants to know what gives him or her the right to talk about us. It comes down to whether people feel they are laughing *with* someone or being the object of someone else's humor.

A situation comes to mind. The day right after Thanksgiving Day is seen by most people as a great day to go shopping. On that day, our sign usually reads:

**ONLY TURKEYS DON'T
GIVE THANKS!**

---

and also

THANKSGIVING HAPPENS

Most pastors I know are very troubled by the increased emphasis on materialistic concerns during the seasons of Advent and Christmas. Somehow the advertisers and retailers have done a very good job of convincing people happiness comes from buying things and giving them. (If you're interested, my shirt size is 17-inch collar and a 37-inch sleeve). I wouldn't recommend making a sign that condemns shoppers or even criticizes them. However, you can make a comment about the need to worship and issue an invitation to do so. This next sign connects a traditional musical term with two composers and also invites people to take note of the opportunity to worship:

GOING CHOPIN?
SPEND SOME MINUETS WITH GOD!
COME BACH TO CHURCH!

This sign was received favorably. Two people quickly sent e-mail messages to me stating their pleasure about the sign. One message read, "I saw your sign and laughed so much, I didn't think I could *Handel* it." The other message said, "I really loved the sign, but I was hoping you would *Lizst* more composers."

Always remember that humor is the servant, the format for drawing attention to the foolishness of the Gospel. "For the foolishness of God is wiser than man's wisdom, and the weakness of God is stronger than man's strength" (1 Corinthians 2:25). This "foolishness" appears throughout the Scriptures and can be translated to your audience by connecting a common phrase with a biblical character and twisting it just a bit. For example, a few years ago, it was popular to confess, "I'm having a bad hair day." While thinking about how I could tap into the popularity of that phrase, a couple of long-haired biblical characters came to mind: Samson and Absalom. Both of them had really bad "hair" days. But then it came to me that one of the most foolish stories of forgiveness is the account of the prodigal son and the waiting father. This son didn't realize the inheritance was already his. So by taking a word similar to *hair*—*heir*—the sign for bad hair days became:

THE PRODIGAL SON
WAS HAVING
A BAD HEIR DAY

More recently, nonprofit organizations that promote taking care of hearts and lungs have called our attention to "air quality." A recent statement about "good air quality" inspired me to write:

THE PRODIGAL SON
DID NOT HAVE
GOOD HEIR QUALITY!

Another popular trend among young people was the "unplugged" concerts promoted by MTV that featured performances by musicians playing acoustical as opposed to electrical guitars. *Unplugged* conveys a sense of being pure, straightforward, and spontaneous. However, unplugged also suggests being disconnected from one's energy source. The tone of our church sign is to be more invitational than confrontational so the sign ended up asking:

UNPLUGGED?
PLUG IN & GET
CURRENT WITH GOD

A good part of the magnetism of this saying is based on the audience knowing about being *unplugged*. Its humor is transformed by playing with the word *current*, because the real energy source is Jesus Christ. The sign is also more positive than negative!

Disastrous floods damaged many communities along the Mississippi and Missouri Rivers in the summer of 1993. During the winter and spring of 1997, the Red River area in states such as Minnesota and North Dakota was devastated by the effects of flood waters. Many church groups worked countless hours to help people protect their businesses, church buildings, and homes. The following sign combines two words that are thought to be negatives—*sandbagging* and *inaction*—and changes them into positives with the addition of the word *love*. This proves true once again Paul's words, "Love does not delight in evil but rejoices with the truth. It always protects, always trusts, always hopes, always perseveres" (1 Corinthians 13:6).

SANDBAGGING:
LOVE IN ACTION

Humor is also in the eye of the beholder. I learned this lesson the hard way. A few years ago there was a dance craze called the "Macarena." The music and dance steps were everywhere. If you turned on the radio or the television, the music was heard and everybody was doing the Macarena. If you went to a baseball stadium or community event, the Macarena was something you were supposed to do. It was almost like shaking hands. Just when little kids to senior citizens were doing the dance, others began to make fun of it, and it was the subject of jokes. So I put a saying on our sign that read:

OUR WORSHIP SERVICES ARE
100% MACARENA FREE!

The response was immediate. A few people called the church office and complained the sign was racist. Folks were disappointed in the church because we appeared to be making a discriminating statement regarding Spanish Americans and Mexican Americans. I was shocked. My intention was to make fun of a dance craze gone wild. In no way did I intend to make a racist statement or to discriminate. Our congregation is very supportive of a mission in Panama. We have had a great deal of contact with people from Central America. I took the sign down as quickly as we received those criticisms because there was the perception that the sign was exclusive and not inclusive.

Some people say, "Perception is reality." Another sign bears the truth of that statement. The Mayor of St. Louis was going to be speaking at a Town Hall meeting hosted by our congregation. I noted on our sign that Mayor Bosley was going to be at church on such and such a date. However, I spelled the Mayor's name incorrectly. Cell phone callers quickly let us know the sign was wrong. I immediately changed the incorrect spelling of the name. It was only up for four hours. However, we received phone calls for four days after the sign had been changed. People were still seeing the mistake in their minds as opposed to the corrected name on the sign. I shared the story with Mayor Bosley, and he told me that sometimes politics is like the experience with the sign. In other words, people see or hear something incorrect and it stays in their minds. Obviously, you want the church sign to help viewers have the "last laugh." This incident and others like it give testimony to the effect of signs. Thousands of people see the message every day. It can be a relevant and inviting or out of touch and demanding message. If you were looking to visit a church for the first time, which church would you try? Use the following checklist to take a visitor's look at your own church. Which church are you?

Exclusive

Judgmental

Legalistic

Tribalistic

Chauvanistic

Inciting

Inflammatory

Degrading

Lifeless

Humorless

Mean

Paternalistic

Maternalistic

Childish

Inclusive

Analytical

Fair

Ethnic (Kiss Me, I'm Swedish)

Open

Insightful

Kindling, enlightening

Uplifting

Life Giving

Joyful

Kind

"Of the Father's Love Begotten"

Motherly (Is.66:13) "As a mother comforts"

Childlike

In other words, does your church pass the 1 Corinthians 13 test? "Love is patient, love is kind. It does not envy, it does not boast, it is not proud. It is not rude, it is not self-seeking, it is not easily angered, it keeps no record of wrongs. Love does not delight in evil but rejoices with truth. It always protects, always trusts, always hopes, always perseveres."

FAX THE PAX

Technology has certainly improved the way we tell the story. Two fairly inexpensive items can help your sign have a wider audience than the people who drive by church: a Polaroid camera and a fax machine. When they are combined with a copier, the sign saying can be sent to just about any place in the world. (The same can be done with a scanner and the congregation's website.) Both tools can be utilized by just about everyone.

Normally, at our church, when the sign is changed (usually on a weekly basis) a Polaroid or two is taken of the sign. It helps to put it in the files (I can't always read my own writing) and more important, if it is a public service announcement or something that I want to share, it can be photocopied and immediately faxed to an organization or agency, newspaper, or radio station. A word of warning: signs about the strawberry festival, while being very important to your congregation and community, might not really be perceived as a news item. I usually reserve the option to send sign sayings to the media until I have something that fits a special category. The last thing you want to do is flood the media with items from your church that don't have a wide appeal. If it is a congratulatory sign, you might want to take a Polaroid and send a card or note to the person or organization that is being recognized. An investment of time in these little things can create or strengthen a bond and pay off with big dividends.

....

WORD

"In the beginning was the Word, and the Word was with God, and the Word was God" (John 1:1). We live in a visually oriented culture. Like doubting Thomas, we have come to the conclusion that seeing is believing. Another insight of an encounter with the resurrected Christ is "believing is seeing." For when we believe, we see all sorts of ways God is alive and at work in the world. The Word, whether it be spoken or written, is still very powerful, despite our world's focus and emphasis on the visual experience. Your church sign can connect with people through just six to eight words.

As people who have been nurtured by the Word, we know and believe it is life-giving. It helps people find direction and purpose in their lives: "Your word is a lamp to my feet and a light for my path" (Psalm 119:105). A church sign can be a beacon of hope and life to those experiencing times of stormy weather.

A Sign for Every Season

Advent

Advent is an invitation to enter into counter-cultural activities. It is an opportunity to become a subversive, to infiltrate, to demonstrate what the reason for the season is all about. It is the celebration of the first coming of Christ as a child in the manger, and how He comes to us through the Word and sacraments and, ultimately, preparation for His return, the second coming of our Lord and Savior Jesus Christ at the end of time.

Advent is my favorite season of the church year because the prayers for each of the four weeks in Advent ask God to stir up things and people. During the other 48 weeks we pray for God to smooth things out, to still the seas that rage around and within us, to calm the storms of life. But for the four weeks of Advent, we ask God to stir up our lives. That's risky business. If I could design liturgical paraments, I'd make sure that all the stoles and altar cloths have an eggbeater on them to represent the "stirring" nature of this time.

The season of Advent is a time to have God mold and shape us according to His values and will. The prophet Isaiah said it so well, "We are the clay, you are the potter; we are all the work of your hand" (Isaiah 64:8). As we get ready for the holidays, we need to remember if you take *holiday* apart, you get "holy day." And the purpose of Advent is to set yourself apart to prepare a place in your heart for the birth of the King of Kings. Advent is a timely wake-up call. There is a certain drowsiness that comes from living in our fast-paced world. Sometimes, we are so busy that as soon as we stop, we drop or maybe we don't stop until we drop.

———

FOCUS ON THE CRECHE
TO LIFT YOUR SPIRITS
DUE TO THE HOLIDAY CRUSH!

———

SHOP TILL YOU DROP?
STAY TILL YOU PRAY!

———

JESUS IS THE REASON
FOR THE SEASON

———

I received a holiday note from my chiropractor, another from my auto mechanic, and still another from our florist. All of them included helpful tips on dealing with the stress of the holiday season. Isn't it curious that getting ready for the greatest gift of all, the Son of God, the Prince of Peace, should be surrounded by so much running around and stress? Someone might ask, "What's wrong with this picture?" Or better yet, "What's right with this picture?"

As I grow older, my memories of Christmas receive almost perfect status in my mind. Consequently, I would like Christmas "presents" to be perfect as well. Therein lies the problem—the whole reason of Advent and Christmas, for the gift of a Savior is because we are not perfect. For all the hopes of a perfect Christmas and "sugarplums dancing" in our consciousness, we need to open ourselves up to the reality that Christmas is for people who are not perfect. I am thoroughly convinced that if the story of our Savior's birth was directed and scripted by Martha Stewart, the intention and results would have been quite different. But, thanks be to God, Christmas is for the imperfect.

I was at a basketball game the first week of December when the person next to me asked, "Are you all ready for Christmas?" I laughed and said, " I still have pumpkins and corn stalks on my porch." She looked at me with eyes that conveyed pity for me. She said quite proudly, "I only have two more things to get and then I will be all done with Christmas." Her words conveyed more than I think she wanted them to because I heard in them a finality before the reality of the event taking place.

As I listened to some of the other conversations of the fans sitting around me, I got the impression that many people were quite caught up in the "have-tos" of the season. I must confess that I was eavesdropping into their private conversations. But what I heard were accounts of busy-ness that filled their days and evenings—but not their hearts—with joy. Sadness overshadowed all the activities of their days. The reason for the season, namely the celebration of the birth of our Lord and Savior Jesus Christ, seemed to be off the screen.

ADVENT—THE PAUSE
THAT REFRESHES!

The words of Isaiah 40:1–2 came to mind , "Comfort, comfort My people, says your God. Speak tenderly to Jerusalem, and proclaim to her that hard service has been completed, that her sin has been paid for, that she has received from the LORD's hand double for all her sins." If I had a Christmas wish, it would be that we could really see the reason for the season—Jesus Christ. This wish would mean that all of us would be "comforted" this season. Not so much in the way we normally think of comfort, with a big pillow and blanket, sitting in an easy chair, munching our favorite comfort food. But truly comforted, put at ease, knowing God sent a Savior for us. Lots of dynamics take place during the holidays. Many feelings get more intense. Some of that is great; some of it is not so great. If you are celebrating the adoption or birth of a little one, the story of Jesus being born in a stable brings it all together. If you are feeling low, sad, and left out, all the joyful singing and ringing of the season seems to be for everyone else but you. The good news is that it is for everyone. There is a comfort in knowing God so loved the world He gave His only Son to die on a cross and rise from the grave.

My Christmas wish would free all of us from the "have-tos" and take us to the land of "get-tos." If baking cookies is your way of sharing the sweetness and joy of the season, then stir up the dough, make and bake them, and deliver them to people who normally don't get to taste the sweetness of the season. If your gift is singing, then make a joyful noise in a place where joyful sounds aren't heard. If your blessing is prayer, then pray for a world that is in such a hurry. If you have the gift of saying kind things or just being with people who are anxious, then bring a sense of wholeness and ease to those who anxious. James exhorted the people: "You too, be patient and stand firm, because the Lord's coming is near" (James 5:8). Those words are difficult for us to hear and see. As I sit at the computer at home or in my office, I want it to work faster than it does. We have instant coffee, fast food, and drive-up windows for banking, film developing, and even mortuaries. Patience is a word and concept our culture has forgotten. And yet, waiting and watching are primary themes for Advent. They are part of a spiritual discipline that helps us live in a world focused on instant gratification.

The church has a great opportunity to help people de-stress during these hectic holidays. We know the reason for the season is Jesus. Now, speaking from past experience there is also a temptation to want to play John the Baptist during this season of excess. I think instead of focusing on excess, it might be more helpful to lift up the idea of access. Church is a place, a community to access the reason for the season. John the Baptist was a one-man spiritual SWAT team. I can only imagine what his church sign would read. The challenge for the writer of the signs during this time of year is how to craft a message that doesn't make the church look like a Grinch or Scrooge. One Advent our sign read:

WELCOME ANGELS, SHEPHERDS,
WISE ONES, EVEN
GRINCHES AND SCROOGES!

I believe that sign is more effective than just listing the themes of Advent like WAIT, WATCH, AND WAKE UP. Those concepts, as valid as they are, appear as commands. Maybe something along the lines of the following would be more enlightening:

FOR A HAPPY NEW YEAR
COME IN AND LEARN HOW
TO BE A HAPPY NEW YOU!

This sign couples the idea of change with the concept that Advent is the beginning of the church year.

CHRISTMAS

KIDS, LEARN CAROLS NOW
YOU HAVE MORE RAM
WHEN YOU'RE A LITTLE LAMB!

"But the angel said to them, 'Do not be afraid. I bring you good news of great joy that will be for all the people. Today in the town of David a Savior has been born to you; He is Christ the Lord. This will be a sign to you: You will find a baby wrapped in cloths and lying in a manger' " (Luke 2:10–12). Several years ago, our family went out a few days before Christmas to do some last-minute shopping. When we returned home there was a yellow note from a delivery service on our door saying, "Sorry we missed you." It listed the options to arrange another time for delivery or pick-up at the warehouse. My wife and I were frustrated because we didn't see how we could find the time to go claim the package. The children were disappointed because they were hoping for some more gifts. We turned the note over and saw a handwritten note, "If you look under the lid of your barbecue grill on your patio, you will find the package." We all ran to the patio. Sure enough, there it was, as promised. During the holy season of Advent and Christmas we celebrate the greatest gift of all, Jesus Christ. Just as we were promised, Jesus is there right for us, for our family, for our friends, for the entire world. In fact, we are claimed by Him in Holy Baptism and marked with the sign of the cross. I encourage you to take all the signs and wonders of this season personally. In other words, take them to heart and rejoice because "unto us a child is born, unto us a son is given."

THE BABY IN THE MANGER
SPELLS OUT GOD'S
TERMS OF ENDEARMENT

Terms of Endearment was a popular movie. A song inspired another sign for these times, "God Is Watching Us":

GOD IS WATCHING US
FROM THE MANGER!

This particular sign emphasized the fact that God is not distant or far away, but rather "The Word became flesh and made His dwelling among us" (John 1:14). Quite often, people ask a preacher if he finds it more difficult to preach a Christmas Eve sermon because he knows there will be lots of visitors present. I always respond to those inquiries by stating the role of the preacher at times is to get out of the way of the story. This story about the baby in the manger is life changing. The church sign at a time like Christmas can help the community give thanks for the greatest gift of all. It is an awesome time to direct people in their thinking. A sign can celebrate:

HOLY FAMILY VALUES
ACCEPTANCE, PONDERING
& BEING STILL!

—

EPIPHANY

In the winter of 1997 a musical group known as the Spice Girls was very popular with adolescent girls. As the season of Epiphany came, I put the following message on the sign:

—

THE MAGI—1ST CENTURY
SPICEBOYS! THEY KNEW BABY
WAS REASON FOR THE SEASON!

—

The Wise Men brought gold, frankincense, and myrrh. They followed the star. It must have been quite a journey. Although I am not a "trekkie," I was aware enough of the fact the space ship on Star Trek was the *Starship Enterprise*. These two terms combined to make a very memorable and popular sign:

—

EPIPHANY:
AN ENTERPRISING
STAR TREK

—

The season of Epiphany (which means a manifestation or revelation) has been described by some as a "spiritual flash" going off in the cosmos. Nestled between the days of Advent/Christmas and Lent, Epiphany coincides with the beginning of a new calendar year. Consequently, it is a time of resolutions. The following sign is invites people to make a new beginning and to work on their resolutions:

IN ORDER TO RE-SOLVE PROBLEMS, GOD IS THE ANSWER & AUTHOR OF NEW YEAR'S RE-SOLUTIONS

The days of Epiphany are excellent to follow the STAR. A popular bumper sticker from years ago read, "Wise Men Still Seek Him." I like the acknowledgment that people are on a spiritual journey, but I would make that statement a little more inclusive to read:

WISE WOMEN, WISE MEN, WISE BOYS, AND WISE GIRLS STILL SEEK HIM! FOLLOW THE STAR!

By being inclusive, we acknowledge that all people can be on a spiritual journey. The star of the Christ Child led some pretty unusual visitors to His manger. Isn't it about time we opened our eyes to see those who hunger and thirst for the Good News of the Star of stars, namely, the Light of the world, Jesus Christ?

The season of Epiphany concludes with the Festival of Transfiguration. This event can be described as a "peek at the peak." "After six days Jesus took with Him Peter, James and John, the brother of James, and led them up a high mountain by themselves. There He was transfigured before them. His face shone like the sun, and His clothes became as white as the light. Just then there appeared before them Moses and Elijah, talking with Jesus" (Matthew 17:1–3). This is the day we sing alleluia for the last time until Easter Sunday.

I remember one Transfiguration Day a few years ago when there was an ice storm. Now that was not too unusual, because Transfiguration comes during winter. What was unusual on that particular Transfiguration Day was the fact that tulips and daffodils were already blossoming and unfolding. The ice storm coated all these beautiful flowers and made them glisten in the sunlight. I thought the scene was an appropriate reminder of the faith and hope we have as Christians because of what Jesus Christ has done for us and continues to do for us. At the same time, the storms of life often come and bring a freezing chill on the warmth of our hearts. Sometimes the spiritual wind chill gets so cold that it is hard to think that spring, much less summer, will ever come again. And yet, there are moments when the sun dances through the icicles hanging on the awning and a rainbow appears. Even though it is frigid outside, there is a momentary relief, a heat wave to the soul.

Transfiguration Day is a time to soak up the glory that exists; a time to rest, relax, and catch our breath. We're at the zenith—the top of the mountain—and in the distance, a little more than 40 days from now, we see another mountain. It is more of a hill, on the far side of town, "where our dear Lord will be crucified, who died to save us all." It's a *peek* at the *peak*!

So we walk slowly down the mountain, knowing that for the next six weeks we are walking in the valley of the shadow of death. A death that means life! It will be on that little mountain where the voice of a Roman Centurion who has seen it all confesses, "Surely this man was the Son of God" (Mark 15:39). Our response can be summed up into just one word as we catch that vision, "Alleluia!"

....

LENT

Trying to describe what the attitude and events of Ash Wednesday and Lent are all about is like going to the doctor after surgery or a biopsy. The doctor shuffles the papers on her desk, looks around the room, and says, "We got the reports back from the lab; it's bad news for you. You have a terminal illness." When those words come out, there is a silence, a shock that is deafening. It is also an awesome task to be the one who presents that sad news. Talking about sin and death is probably the last taboo in our culture. You can turn on any TV station and the discussion will be about all sorts of things we didn't even whisper about in private. Now it seems everything is out in the open, everything except an honest discussion about mortality. Right before Ash Wednesday 1998, I put the following verse from a nursery rhyme on our sign:

ASHES, ASHES
WE ALL FALL DOWN!

This particular sign received a great deal of discussion. It connected to many people who were aware of its origin as a rhyme about the plagues in the Middle Ages. It also caught people's attention and helped them focus on the Ash Wednesday experience.

Ash Wednesday is a day to deal with the whole issue of sins and the consequences of our thoughts and actions. It is a day to pray to God, "Have mercy on me, O God, according to your unfailing love, according to your great compassion blot out my transgressions" (Psalm 51:1). Or in 90s language, "In Your great compassion delete my transgressions from the file, purge me from my sin, and I will be pure." These words form the basis of King David's prayer, which he wrote after he was confronted by Independent Counsel Nathan the Prophet, regarding his participation in Bathsheba-gate. It is still quite appropriate for us, "Create in me a pure heart, O God, and renew a steadfast spirit within me" (Psalm 51:10).

"Create in me a clean heart ..." this prayer (written long before cholesterol counts and angioplasty) is centered on having a center (heart) centered on the center of all life—God. As the prophet Joel proclaimed in the middle of a terrible supernatural disaster, " 'Even now,' declares the LORD, 'return to Me with all your heart, with fasting and with weeping and mourning.' Rend your heart and not your garments. Return to the LORD your God, for He is gracious and compassionate, slow to anger and abounding in love" (Joel 2:12–13). This is the God who made all this come true in the life, death, and resurrection of Jesus Christ. This call to repentance inspired a favorite sign for the season:

LENT:
U-TURNS PERMITTED
AND ENCOURAGED

Create in me a clean heart O God and *renew* a right steadfast spirit within me. This raises the whole issue of Lent as a time of renewal—a time to get your batteries re-charged, to give up some things, and also take on some new things. To get connected—if you are feeling disconnected—to simplify if you feel overwhelmed, to return, if you feel you have wandered away.

The Lenten season usually coincides with the beginning of spring training for baseball. As sports call-in radio shows discuss the upcoming season, there is a sense of new beginnings, of hope, of being very focused on the goal. In order to achieve your goal, serious workouts are necessary. Individuals and teams practice and perform basic drills so they might get in shape for opening day. The season of Lent came about a long time before spring training, but it is similar. Lent is a time to work on our skills and abilities so we might accomplish our goal of sharing Christ with the nations.

LENT
IS SPRING TRAINING
FOR CHRISTIANS!

It is also a time to patch up relationships. One day the street department was working on the potholes near our church. I realized that's exactly what Lent is all about. It is a time to fill in those areas that need it.

LENT:
A TIME TO FILL IN
THE POTHOLES OF LIFE!

Many churches offer extra opportunities for prayer, study, and worship during Lent. It is helpful to make note of these on your sign. Our congregation sponsored a parenting workshop during Lent. Our sign was an invitation to people to attend:

PARENTING WORKSHOP
LENTEN "TOOL TIME"
FOR HOME IMPROVEMENT!

Some of the humor and name recognition of this particular sign is built on the popularity of a television program called "Home Improvement" that features a cable show called "Tool Time." In the United States, tax preparation time usually coincides with some of the Lenten season. Ideas like *audit*, *report*, *deductions*, and *return* are on the minds of many people. A sign that relates to this common experience but also connects to a biblical truth could read something like:

WE OFFER COUNSEL
SO YOU ARE NOT AUDITED
ON YOUR FINAL RETURN!

DEDUCT SIN EXEMPTIONS
FROM YOUR
SPIRITUAL 1040 FORM.

TO MAKE TAX TIME
LESS TAXING
REFUNDS ACCEPTED HERE!

Holy Week is the culmination of many feelings and emotions. For several years it seems to have coincided with the Final Four NCAA Basketball Tournament. One of the marketing slogans for college basketball is "March Madness." That particular slogan coupled with a sense of the passion and mystery of this Holy Week prompts several different signs:

MARCH MADNESS:
IN LIKE A LION
OUT LIKE A LAMB!

WE DON'T READ PALMS;
WE WAVE THEM!

HOLY WEEK
A WEEK OF
A WAKE!

One year, Good Friday was April Fool's Day. This day of foolishness and trickery reminded me of a song, "The Fool on the Hill," so our sign simply read:

THE FOOL ON THE HILL
IS THERE FOR
YOU & ME!

A good friend of mine, who travels a great deal because of business, suggested this sign for Maundy Thursday and Good Friday:

PASSENGERS AND CREW,
THE CAPTAIN STATES
"PREPARE FOR CROSS CHECK"

EASTER

"He is risen! He is risen, indeed!" That call and response is an ancient greeting still shared today. As the cheers of Palm Sunday quickly turn into jeers and accusations, as the "Hosannas" are drowned out by chants of "Crucify Him," we watch and wait and have hope. For we know as a popular radio spokesman says, "The Rest of the Story." Easter is the rest of the story and it changes our life stories. This past year on Easter Sunday, our sign read:

WE'RE OPEN EASTER SUNDAY
BECAUSE THE TOMB
WAS OPEN EASTER SUNDAY!

"For as in Adam all die, so in Christ all shall be made alive" (1 Corinthians 15:22). Another Easter sign that was very popular was based on the concept of the Spice Girls and Luke 24:1 and 10, "On the first day of the week, very early in the morning, the women took spices they had prepared and went to the tomb. ... It was Mary Magdalene, Joanna, Mary the mother of James, and the others with them who told this to the apostles." This sign added some flavor to the Easter season:

JOANNA, MARY, &
MARY MAGDALENE
THE ORIGINAL SPICE GIRLS!

A colorful sign is based on the homophones *die* and *dye*:

EASTER:
MORE THAN SOMETHING
TO DYE FOR!

One day, just a few days after Easter Sunday, I went for a quick walk around the park in my neighborhood. In an effort to burn off calories (from all those chocolate eggs and jelly beans), reduce stress, and get some exercise, I was focused on my pace, breathing, and moving my arms in order to maximize the aerobic event. I was over halfway through my walk when I saw a little boy who had wandered away from the playground. In a cheerful voice he said, "Hi!" Not wanting to really make a connection, I didn't give eye contact, kept walking, and said a very curt, "Hi."

But the little boy was not to be denied. In an angelic voice he called out to me, "Ain't it a sunny day!"

His proclamation stopped me dead in my tracks. Yes, it sure was, but I hadn't seen it, enjoyed it, or most important of all, given thanks for it. As I picked up the pace, I rounded a bend and there in front of me was the most beautiful purple tree full of blossoms. I don't think I have ever seen a more glorifying example of Martin Luther's words, "The message of the resurrection is not written in books alone, but in every leaf of springtime."

I don't know if it can be proven from a scientific, medical, or technical point of view that there is a direct connection between your heart and your eyes. I mean if you look at the charts in medical books or the graphics on a medical CD-ROM, I don't think there is a cable that connects what's in the heart with what's in your eyes. But, in spiritual terms, the connection, the network is obvious.

As the two disciples made their way to Emmaus on Easter Sunday evening, they encountered the risen Christ. The three walked and talked all the way to their destination. However, it wasn't until the breaking of bread, "their eyes were opened and they recognized Him" (Luke 24:30). As Jesus took the bread and blessed it, their eyes were opened and, consequently, their cardiac condition changed as well. They went from burning and aching hearts to hearts on fire for the Lord. In other words, believing is seeing.

Thomas the Twin, AKA "doubting Thomas" is one of the best examples of experiencing the phenomenon of believing is seeing. Initially, Thomas doubted, and it wasn't until he received proof, the information he requested, that he was able to believe. It is traditional in many churches that the story of doubting Thomas is read the Sunday after Easter. For years, we have utilized the following message on that Sunday:

DOUBTERS WELCOME!

As you can imagine, we receive a few comments about that particular sign. Some of my members asked me, "Pastor, are you promoting doubt?" And my answer is "No, I am not promoting doubt. It seems to happen without much encouragement. But what I am doing is recognizing the fact that many people who have doubt don't feel like they can come to church. Their perception is that church is only for people who have all the answers. We want to invite people to experience Jesus who is 'the Way, the Truth and the Life' (John 14).

There are seven weeks of Easter. It is a time of 50 days to celebrate and recognize, "this is the day the LORD has made; let us rejoice and be glad in it" (Psalm 118:24). Several of the Sundays during Easter focus attention on Jesus as the Good Shepherd. One year during this season our sign read:

___

CAN'T SLEEP?
COUNTING SHEEP?
TALK TO THE SHEPHERD!

___

Another sign around this time of year read:

___

WE'RE NOT PULLING THE
WOOL OVER YOUR EYES!
JESUS IS THE GOOD SHEPHERD

___

I remember going to church about 40 years ago and looking at the cradle roll in the narthex. There were all these little lambs connected to the Good Shepherd. Each child in the congregation had his or her name on a little lamb. If I remember correctly, there was quite a flock of sheep, and in good Lutheran fashion, all the little boy lambs were separate from all the little girl lambs. Little blue ribbons connected the little boy lambs and little pink ribbons connected the little girl lambs. I distinctly remember standing there looking for my name and feeling a sense of belonging, "The LORD is my shepherd, I shall not be in want" (Psalm 23:1).

While city dwellers don't have too many encounters with

sheep or shepherds, there is a high recognition of the shepherd image. It is good news for *baaad* times. Forty days after Easter, Ascension Day takes place. This day, while not widely celebrated, is a wonderful time to create an uplifting message on the church sign. Two of my favorite Ascension Day signs are guaranteed to have your viewers looking up:

ASCENSION DAY
IT'S AN UP THING!

This sign is based on the obvious fact that it is an up thing. However, there is also a very popular soft drink that markets it product with the tag line, "It's An Up Thing." The other sign that brings smiles is:

ASCENSION DAY—WHAT GOES UP
WILL COME DOWN
IT'S GRACE NOT GRAVITY.

"They were looking intently up into the sky as He was going, when suddenly two men dressed in white stood beside them. 'Men of Galilee,' they said, 'why do you stand here looking into the sky? This same Jesus, who has been taken from you into heaven, will come back in the same way you have seen Him go into heaven'" (Acts 1:14).

....

PENTECOST

Pentecost is for dreamers. The prophet Joel proclaimed the Word of the Lord, "I will pour out My Spirit on all people. Your sons and daughters will prophesy, your old men will dream dreams, your young men will see visions" (Joel 2:28). Pentecost is for dreamers. It is a day to give thanks to God for His wonderful blessings. Originally, it was day commemorating the 50th day after the barley was cut. Pentecost was a celebration of God's gifts of rain and sunshine, which enabled the crops to grow. Coupled with the thanksgiving motif was one of inclusiveness. On this day the Jews celebrated the gift of the Torah. Tradition had it that when the Law was given, it was given in all the languages of the world, thus demonstrating God is the God of all people, the Lord and King of the universe. On that Pentecost Day in A.D. 33, when all the people could hear their own language being proclaimed, it was a powerful message, a dream come true.

Dreams are a wonderful gift from God. God sends us messages, and we receive them, though sometimes we don't know what they mean. At other times we can't even remember them. And yet, at special times, these messages change our lives, our way of thinking, living, and loving. Throughout the Bible, people were touched by dreams from God. We remember young Joseph, who had dreams and could also interpret them. Abimelech, Jacob, Laban, Daniel, and Peter were also recipients of dreams. Pentecost is for dreamers, for people who have experienced nightmares. For folks who have chased their dreams only to find out that they were illusions or mirages. Pentecost isn't deception, but reception of the Spirit of God. Pentecost calls us to dream, to have visions, to see things that others don't see. The Light of the World calls us to find our way. We are called to call others to realize that sunsets do happen, but we know there is a dawn waiting for us. That's the dream, that's Pentecost.

———

PENTECOST
THE ORIGINAL
MISSION POSSIBLE!

———

Pentecost is the birthday party of the church. For several years, I have put the following message on our sign around the Festival of Pentecost:

———

UNDER THE SAME MANAGEMENT
SINCE PENTECOST A.D. 33

———

This sign has received very positive comments and also very

critical comments. The positive comments are based on an understanding that Christian churches have their roots and basis in the history of the early church. The negative comments stem from branches of Christianity that emphasize almost a monopolistic understanding of God's spirit and love. I think this particular sign has been misunderstood to be saying, "The Lutheran Church has been around since A.D. 33." I have been surprised by the heat of the correspondence from people who state they have the warmth of Christ in their hearts. Even though the sign has been misunderstood by a few, I keep using it because I think it is effective to a larger audience.

Most avid cyclists carry several items on their bikes. Included on the necessary list of equipment is a set of tools for some quick repair jobs, some spare change to purchase drinks, a patch kit, including an inner tube, and most important of all, an air pump! A cyclist can have all the hi-tech gadgets, he or she can be wearing the last cycling fashions, but if the cyclist doesn't have enough air in the tires, the journey comes to an end or might not even be started. I have a little routine that I do before each ride. Part of this ritual includes checking the air pressure in the tires.

The Festival of Pentecost is a fabulous day to celebrate the gift of the Holy Spirit who, as Martin Luther wrote, "calls, gathers, enlightens and sanctifies the whole Christian Church." Much has been written in recent years about volunteerism. Many people see the church as just another volunteer organization. While part of that designation is helpful in terms of care and nurturing of volunteers, it is most important to remember the church is a community of people who have been called out of the world by the Holy Spirit. It is also very important to have our air pressure checked from time to time.

OUT OF BREATH?
GET PUMPED UP WITH
SPIRITUAL CPR—FREE AIR!

THE PRODIGAL SON HAD
LOW HEIR PRESSURE.
FILL UP WITH THE RIGHT SPIRIT!

———

The season of Pentecost is the longest of the church year, approximately five months long, going from late springtime through summer, into the fall. During these times, there are many opportunities to enlighten and entertain. My advice is to be aware of the various calendars that exist in the minds of individuals. For example, the beginning of the school year runs from September through late May or even June. The church year goes from the first Sunday in Advent through Christ the King Sunday (51 weeks later). The New Year begins January 1. Obviously, if you live in a community where a particular sport garners a lot of attention, it is important to be cognizant of those interests and schedules.

Secular Holidays

This is one of the more interesting and creative oxymorons, (two opposite words matched together) like *jumbo shrimp, plastic silverware, paid volunteers*. Secular Holy Days dot everyone's calendars. The Fourth of July prompted the following sign:

———

LITANY FIREWORKS?
SPARK YOUR FAITH &
HAVE A BLAST IN LIFE!

———

If you aren't sure which days seem to be secular holidays, just stop, look, and listen! You'll figure it out.

THE GOSPEL ACCORDING TO HOLLYWOOD

REEL LIFE OR REAL LIFE?

A very rich source of messages for signs can be found in Hollywood movies. Advertising proclaims the upcoming arrival of a new film and literally saturates the senses. Accompanying these ads are related marketing campaigns with fast food restaurants. Even children who can't read already know the title of a new movie and what kind of action figure they can get when their parents buy a meal for them.

Because movies are so popular and the advertising campaigns are so intentional and intensive, the title of a movie is often on the minds of most people. Consequently, many folks will recognize a sign that refers to a movie. Remember, while there may be story content or language that is offensive, movies can be described as being descriptive or prescriptive. That is, they can be an accurate portrayal or how people act in a world broken by sin. A movie whose title summarized what it was all about was *An Indecent Proposal*. The premise of the movie became the subject of discussions on talk radio and also around the office water cooler. Rather than propose something indecent, church is always positioning people to behave decently. Thus, the sign:

———

A DECENT PROPOSAL:
FORGIVE AS WE
HAVE BEEN FORGIVEN

———

Sometimes, a movie can also be prescriptive, stating how we could and should act in particular situations:

———

MOVIES—REEL LIFE
THE BIBLE—REAL LIFE
STILL THE BEST SELLER

———

TIRED OF PULP FICTION?
BE ENERGIZED BY
THE WORD OF TRUTH

———

I remember a very significant scene in the movie *Places in the Heart* that conveyed a beautiful message of what the body of Christ looks like when forgiveness is offered and received. The real transformation grace brings is reel transportation via some thoughtful and poignant movies. The following sign linked two separate movies that were nominated for Academy Awards:

———

UNFORGIVEN?
CRYING GAME?
JESUS DIED FOR YOU!

———

The release dates of movies is also something to consider. Many movies are released right before Christmas and at the beginning of the summer. The sequel to the movie *Terms of Endearment* came out right before Christmas. The following sign just seemed to say it all:

THE BABY IN THE MANGER
SPELLS OUT GOD'S
TERMS OF ENDEARMENT

This particular sign appeared in the local newspaper and was frequently mentioned during the holiday season.

One of the favorite signs of many children has its foundation in a movie about cartoon characters Wilma and Fred Flintstone:

A BEDROCK FAITH
YABBA-DABBA-DO
GOD LOVES YOU!

Bedrock is the name of the community where the characters live. It also reminds us that God is a fortress, a rock (see Psalm 46). Another popular movie was *Home Alone 2*. During its release, the sign read:

HOME ALONE 2?
COME TOGETHER
AT CHURCH

This sign plays on the words *two, too,* and *to*. Using the numeral reduces a few letters and also follows the name of the movie. It is also an invitation to come to church. Many people perceive church to be for families. If one is alone at home, he or she certainly doesn't want to be alone at church too. Church is a place where people come together and find community.

Movie character Forrest Gump was fond of saying, "Mama always said, 'life is like a box of chocolates.' " The phrase became very popular. People of all ages were using it in conversations. Consequently, the following sweet message was offered:

CHURCH IS LIKE
A BOX OF CHOCOLATES ...

You never really know how certain signs will affect people. This particular sign was criticized by one woman. She wrote me a letter saying that the sign had offended her because her daughter had a health problem that did not allow her to eat candy. In the woman's mind, this sign was exclusive. Her rationale was, "If church is like a box of chocolates and someone can't eat candy, then this church isn't accepting of someone in that particular situation." I was quite surprised by this critique. In reality, I am sure it probably had more to do with this woman's own feelings than with the sign itself. However, I contacted the woman and assured her we were not intending to be exclusive. Rather, we wanted to be very inclusive. This is an important point. While I don't think my call changed her mind, I responded with poise, compassion, and in a professional manner. What's most important is what story the sign is sharing. I want the sign to remind people about the sweetness of the Good News as opposed to leaving a sour taste in their minds.

DO YOU HAVE A TITANIC
SINKING FEELING? HOPE
WILL FLOAT YOUR BOAT!

The Academy Awards are very popular. Many radio stations and several newspapers offer contests to select the winners. A great deal of attention is paid to the movies at this time of year. It so happens that one year *Dead Man Walking* was nominated for several awards. Easter weekend preceded the Academy Awards that year. Another event, the spring time change also took place that weekend. A combination of those three events was summarized on our sign:

SPRING FORWARD
DEAD MAN RISEN
ALLELUIA!

A little phrase people use to remind themselves which way to turn their clocks is "spring forward, fall back." "Dead man risen" made great sense. And, of course, the Alleluia says it all!

One can build on the name recognition of movies and add a little twist to them. In the winter of 1997, there were two very popular films, *Good Will Hunting* and *As Good as it Gets*. These blockbusters developed into a wonderful idea for a sign:

WE TEACH GOOD WILL HUNTING
AND THIS IS NOT
AS GOOD AS IT GETS

Two other movies also were combined to describe the Bible:

THE BIBLE—WRITTEN ON
THE WINGS OF A DOVE AND
QUOTES THE APOSTLE

"All Scripture is God-breathed and is useful for teaching, rebuking, correcting and training in righteousness" (2 Timothy 3:16):

THE BIBLE
WHEN READ AND APPLIED
MAKES DEEP IMPACT!

TOPICAL SIGNS

People have told me they love the messages on the Gethsemane Church sign because they are so timely. I think it might be fair to say that the typical church sign is internally focused, whereas a sign that strives to enlighten and entertain is externally focused. The Gethsemane sign is more topical than typical. There are all kinds of thoughts, ideas, songs, pieces, and parts of information that come our way. By connecting something that is going on in the world with the Word, the message of the sign can make a difference in the lives the readers. A good friend of mine sent me a letter, in which he noted:

———

THE FIRST ROAD SIGN
WAS THE BURNING BUSH
WHAT'S HOT IN YOUR LIFE?

———

That is the perfect question to ask, "What's hot?" or "What's a burning issue taking place in your community at this time?" I am often asked how I come up with ideas for the signs. My answer is they usually come to me after I spend some time thinking about topics currently being discussed, events taking place, developing themes in the conversations of people. For example, as this book is being written, the 1998 World Cup Soccer championship is taking place. As soccer becomes a more popular sport in North America, there are more and more folks following the World Cup games. By taking the phrase "World Cup" and reversing the order, it could be "Cup for the World." Churches often talk about the uniting aspects of the Lord's Supper. Jesus offers the "Cup for the World" as He calls us to eat and drink in remembrance of Him. If one adds the topic of goal to the phrase, "Cup for the World," it could look something like:

**OUR GOAL ON SUNDAYS
IS TO CELEBRATE THE
CUP FOR THE WORLD!**

In the spring and summer of 1998, there was a heavenly exhibit at the St. Louis Art Museum, "Angels from the Vatican." A great deal of promotion on radio, television, and in the newspapers had taken place before our sign conveyed a message relating to the event. I listed things associated with angels: harps, halos, wings, clouds, heavenly beings, guardian angels. If possible, I like to incorporate an invitation into the message. So the idea of "wing on over" seemed to be a good place to start. And then, building on the invitation of "wing on over," which is "heavenly advice," it became, "Heavenly advice: Wing on over to the Art Museum. " Now that is a pretty good sign, but I added another line to set it off just a bit, to bring a smile to readers' faces. Now the complete sign read:

**HEAVENLY ADVICE: WING ON OVER
TO THE ART MUSEUM
AND SAY, "HALO!"**

TRENDS

Mergers, corporate downsizings, cellular phones, and e-mail all remind us we live in a sea of change. These waves come crashing upon the shores of our life every day. In order to catch the wave, be aware of various trends in everyday life. When comedian David Letterman was switching networks our sign read:

TRY THE LETTERMAN
OF THE BIBLE:
ST. PAUL

This particular sign was based on the fact that Paul authored numerous epistles and was the "Letter Man" of the Bible. During a time when a nationally known online service was having difficulty during peak times in "connecting" all of its clients, our church sign reminded people:

DOWNLOAD YOUR
WORRIES;
GET ON-LINE
WITH GOD

A few years ago, bungee jumping was very popular. Every time you turned on the television or opened the newspaper, there were stories about jumpers of every age. County fairs and amusement parks were advertising opportunities and venues to make a jump. I heard several people say, "I don't think I could do that leap of faith." As soon as I heard those words, I knew our sign needed to state:

NO BUNGEE CORDS,
BUT WE ENCOURAGE
LEAPS OF FAITH!

When Pepsi began a highly promoted campaign featuring Ray Charles and the "Uh-Huh" Girls, there was a great deal of speculation about the "secret" ingredient in this particular beverage. Every place you went there were people saying and singing "Uh-Huh." In following Paul's great insights about love in 1 Corinthians 13, it was very refreshing to disclose:

THE REAL SECRET
INGREDIENT
IS LOVE—UH HUH!

Around the same time there was a trend involving *clear*. Soft drinks and other products were marketed with a particular focus on being *clear*. This sign message simply *bubbled* up one day:

CRYSTAL CLEAR
GOSPEL HERE!

The spring of 1998 marked several mergers among major corporations. As these businesses were bought and sold, I thought it was a good idea to take "stock" in the similarities between banking and religion. There are bonds, an emphasis on fidelity, serious interests in trust, checks, and balances, saving, and most important of all, redemption. I consolidated these ideas for this sign message:

PRAYER IS MERGER TALK
WITH GOD & YOU.
BUILD A BOND, INVEST NOW!

At the same time there was a great deal of interest in a Powerball lottery game. I feel one of the most unfortunate areas of silence on behalf of Christian churches in North America is our culture's thirst for gambling. With a few exceptions, most churches have stood on the sidelines as games of chance have taken over the playing fields of our communities. The media intentionally celebrate instant "winners" while neglecting to report on the devastating effects compulsive gambling has on individuals, their families, employers, and communities. Billboard after billboard entices people to become *winners*! It seems to me the clear message of the Gospel is that Jesus is for losers, "For whoever wants to save his life will lose it, but whoever loses his life for Me will find it" (Matthew 16:25). It's a safe bet the following signs make people think about this trend:

GAMBLING
WHEEL OF MIS-FORTUNE

———

SOLVE THE PUZZLE WITH PRAYER

———

WHEN THE CHIPS ARE DOWN
GOD IS THERE TO LIFT YOU UP!

———

WE DON'T HAVE POWERBALL TICKETS
BECAUSE WITH GOD,
YOU'RE A NAME, NOT A NUMBER!
YOU CAN BET YOUR LIFE!

———

When the Rolling Stones came to St. Louis in 1997, the theme of their tour was "Bridges to Babylon." I think most people who heard the theme didn't even associate Babylon with a place of captivity and exile. I wrote a message whose foundation is God who is "like a rock." This sign was very popular:

———

ROLLING STONES BRIDGES TO
BABYLON! GOD—SOLID ROCK
A BRIDGE TO PROMISED LAND!

———

The sign would have been better without so many letters on each line. The content of the sign was excellent, but it wasn't very easy to read.

A highly rated and successful television program, "ER" (about life in an emergency room) did a live show. In the early days of television, most shows were done live. It seems to me that one of the exciting aspects of worship is that it is performed live every Sunday, and the majority of people who do it are not professionals. Consequently, occasional mistakes are made—the sound quality is not always the greatest, but corporate worship is still the best show in town. We invite people to worship so they can experience the live-ness of the Living Word, Jesus Christ.

**IF YOU HAVE "ER"–RED
EXPERIENCE FORGIVENESS
LIVE ON SUNDAYS!**

Princess Diana and Mother Theresa died within a week of each other. These two women lived and worked in totally different worlds, and the entire world grieved for them. Despite the obvious contrast in lifestyles, both women touched those normally considered untouchable or outcasts. The sign message that week was intended to remind people, "Weeping may remain for a night, but rejoicing comes in the morning" (Psalm 30:5):

**A CANDLE IN THE WIND,
A LIGHT IN THE DARK
REFLECT LOVE FROM ABOVE!**

....

SPORTS

I remember as a child hearing humorous comments like, "Did you know baseball is mentioned in the Bible? Yes, *in the beginning!*" Or, "Did you know tennis is mentioned in the Bible? Yes, Joseph served in Pharaoh's courts." Sports is big business in our world today. Millions of people watch sports on television, listen to games on the radio, and participate weekly and weakly in sports. When the Super Bowl Game is on, it is best not to schedule the congregation's annual meeting. I remember trying to conduct a Stewardship Drive one year as the Kansas City Royals made their way to the World Series. It seemed we couldn't get to *first base* with anyone and we nearly *struck out*. Fortunately, several people did *step up to the plate*, (and also put money in the offering plate) and we met our goal.

In many communities, it isn't professional sports that capture the attention of the fans, but rather high school or college sports. By utilizing the church sign as an illuminated Post-it note, you can cheer on the efforts of amateurs in the community. You can help people take a *seventh-inning stretch* and be refreshed by offering spiritual exercises. When the St. Louis community rallied together to bring a professional football team to town we celebrated with this sign message:

***

TOUCHDOWN!
WELL DONE!
FANS INC!

***

A picture of this sign appeared on the front page of *The Orange County Register* along with a photo from a Los Angeles restaurant, featuring LACK OF RAM! In order to provide financial support for the team, PSLs (Personal Seat Licenses) were sold to interested fans. Some of these PSLs were quite expensive. Intense marketing was done for weeks and everyone was talking about the concept of buying seats for the games. That seemed to me a wonderful opportunity to explain how the church is different from professional sports:

***

THE CHURCH IS
A PSL:
PEOPLE-SERVING-LOVING

***

Another time during a promotional campaign for luxury boxes, we welcomed fans by stating:

***

OUR LUXURY BOXES
ARE FREE!

***

One of the critiques of churches and non-profit organizations is that we are always asking for money. And yet, I rarely hear people express concern about the high price of tickets or being a subscriber to a cable sports network. One year during the playoffs for the NHL Stanley Cup Finals, the St. Louis Blues offered a "pay-per-view" package for their fans. We immediately countered with:

HOCKEY PLAYOFF
SPECIAL
FREE PRAY PER PEW!

There has been an increased interest in automobile racing. When a new track opened up in our area, it received national attention. Our sign message invited people:

ON THE RACE TRACK OF LIFE
MAKE PIT STOPS
PRAY-INSPIRE-TOUCH!

Super Bowl Sunday is one of the secular holidays of the year. It has been said that it is the ultimate game or the "game of the century," but it is played on an annual basis. Some folks watch the game in order to see the commercials. These advertisements receive a great deal of attention prior to the game and certainly after the game. We usually do a couple of signs about the Super Bowl:

OUR SUPER SUNDAY WORSHIP
IS COMMERCIAL FREE!
HEAR THE WORD FROM OUR SPONSOR

EVERY SUNDAY
HERE
IS SUPER SUNDAY

When the Professional Golfers Association (PGA) came to our area for a major golf tournament we made a "hole in one" with:

PGA:
PRAISE
GOD
ALWAYS

This message seemed to really make sense to golfers who have made bogeys, ended up in sand or water traps, and strive to be lifted up as on "wings of an eagle." Perhaps the most famous sign we ever did involved a singer of the National Anthem at a baseball game. When Roseanne Barr "sang" for the San Diego Padres it received a great deal of attention. We noted the event with:

**ROSEANNE BARR
DOESN'T SING HERE,
BUT YOU CAN!**

Whenever there is a big game between one of the local teams and a visiting team, we invite visiting fans to church:

**49ERS' FANS
ARE WELCOME HERE!**

During one of the Olympic Games, the network broadcasting the games invited viewers to "Share a moment with the world." I took that theme and changed it just a bit in order to read:

**AN OLYMPIC IDEA:
SHARE A MOMENT
WITH THE WORD!**

After all, baseball and tennis are biblical:

**BASEBALL IS BIBLICAL!
IN THE BEGINNING!**

**TENNIS IS BIBLICAL
JOSEPH SERVED IN
PHARAOH'S COURTS**

POLITICS

Washington University in St. Louis has been the site for presidential debates. For weeks prior to these scheduled events there is little else on the minds of local residents. One election year when the debate was cancelled, our sign read:

_____

THERE IS NO DEBATE!

GOD LOVES YOU.

_____

It is inappropriate to use the church sign to endorse political candidates or specific referendums (pro or con). Due to the nature of the church's 501c3 status, it is best not to lobby residents to vote in a certain way. However, it is very appropriate to remind voters to vote. The first time our sign emphasized voting, it was done in this manner:

_____

BAD PEOPLE

ARE ELECTED BY GOOD PEOPLE

WHO DON'T VOTE!

_____

I have mixed feelings about this particular sign. I believe it is a true statement. I also know voter apathy is a very important issue in our country. However, this sign does seem to be based a little too much on shame or even name-calling. A revised version of the sign is:

_____

VOTE

VOICE OF THE ELECTORATE

JUST DO IT!

_____

During a different election year, I wrote a sign that mentioned a "four-letter" word. Now, *word* is a four-letter word, but usually when that specific term is used, we think of words inappropriate in conversation, and most certainly inappropriate for sign messages. However, I took the plunge and wrote:

VOTE IS A
FOUR-LETTER WORD.
HANDLE WITH PRAYER

This sign utilizes the "shock" effect. Normally, "four-letter" words aren't on the church sign, except words like, love, hope, care, life, join, and save. Supreme Court rulings are opportunities to speak to the community in a very civil manner. A local community went to the Supreme Court regarding the use of signs in the yards of residents. A resident placed a sign in her yard protesting some military action. According to the laws of that particular community, this was illegal. The case received a great deal of local and even national attention. I wrote the following sign, in a sense to "tweak" the consciousness of the community:

**AREN'T YOU GLAD
THIS SIGN ISN'T
IN LADUE? WE ARE!**

As discussions and debates continue around the practice of school prayer, it is very important to announce to the community that:

**PRAYERS ARE STILL
LEGAL HERE!**

INSPIRATION

Before I ever came to Gethsemane Lutheran, Signmeister Don Sandberg created one of the funniest signs I have ever seen. He wrote:

**WE ARE THE LUTHERANS
GARRISON KEILLOR
IS TALKING ABOUT!**

I know he wrote that sign because he kept a record of all the messages put up since the church purchased the sign. This is a great practice to begin. Inspiration from previous signs often comes because the sign sets a mood or climate and helps, you think about making a sign that enlightens and entertains. I receive inspiration for signs from Scripture. I truly believe God has given me the gift of humor. I also need to quickly add, it has taken me about four decades to learn how to unwrap this gift and share it so it is truly a present to those around me. There was a time when I used humor to keep people at arm's length. I would like to say that I always know the best way to use this gift, but as in the case of all gifts, it is something in process with me.

Commercials and movies are excellent sources of inspiration. You can't help but pick up themes from these highly visual and intentional artistic creations. A popular radio personality, Charles Brennan on KMOX in St. Louis began a campaign to *save* a character for a local bank. A national bank had purchased Boatmen's Bank. So Mr. Brennan was concerned this spokesman, known as the Boatmen's Guy, would not be *saved* but would be *cashed in*. A letter-writing campaign was established to "Help Save the Boatmen's Guy." As soon as I heard that phrase, I knew we wanted to join in the venture because *saving* is what we are all about. So I wrote the sign message:

—

WE WANT TO HELP SAVE
THE BOATMEN'S GUY
& EVERYONE ELSE, TOO!

—

After the message was placed on our sign, I took a picture of the sign and faxed it to Mr. Brennan. He mentioned it on his morning talk show. In addition, it was quoted in the *St. Louis Post-Dispatch* and also the *American Banker*. The bottom line of this story is when you calculate all the attention given to this sign, which didn't cost any church dollars but created lots of interest and made sense to everyone who saw it, celebrate the good investment it was. Following the purchase of this particular bank, the trust department was sold and spun off to another entity. This action prompted our message:

> ———
>
> **CHURCH—WE HAVE**
> **A TRUST DEPARTMENT**
> **YOU CAN BANK ON!**
>
> ———

A country western singer increased the cardiac palpitations of many when he sang about "Achy Breaky Heart." It was very natural to go to the heart of the matter and proclaim:

> ———
>
> **ACHY BREAKY HEARTS**
> **ARE**
> **HEALED AT CHURCH**
>
> ———

Inspiration for signs is everywhere. All one needs to do is stop, look, and listen to the "din" around us. For in those sights and sounds, in the messages, there are phrases and ideas that can be utilized to call attention to the holiest message of all—God's love in the life, death, and resurrection of Jesus Christ.

PUBLIC SERVICE ANNOUNCEMENTS

Christians are in the world but not of the world. Quite often congregations, when asked what their mission is, will answer with the words of Matthew 28:20, we want to "go and make disciples of all nations, baptizing them in the name of the Father and of the Son and of the Holy Spirit." However, having made that profession, which has global implications, the same leaders in a congregation will behave as if they aren't members of the neighborhood or community where their church is. So when the president of the neighborhood association calls and asks the church to put the notice of the 52-neighborhood family rummage sale (proceeds will benefit an after-school latchkey program) on the church sign, the response is often a curt *no*. Or even worse, a long negative answer filled with complaints and accusations.

The church sign can be a bridge to the community or it can be a wall. By utilizing the high visibility of the church sign, a congregation can support (quite effortlessly) events and activities in the community. A bridge helps people cross over from one side to the other side. A wall can and does shut people out.

A public service announcement accomplishes things. First, you are saying "we care about this community, the people in this place." Second, we care about something other than ourselves. Churches are often criticized for being inwardly oriented. When we care for others, we are doing what Jesus called us to do. Matthew 25 is a wonderful testimony to the call to have "evangelical eyes," to see Jesus in the people whom we serve.

When you're contemplating PSAs, don't wait until you're asked—take the initiative and do it on your own. Highlight the blood drive being sponsored by the local hospital or school.

WE WANT NEGATIVE
& POSITIVE PEOPLE.
BLOOD DRIVE

WE NEED YOUR TYPE!
SUPPORT THE BLOOD DRIVE
SATURDAY, NOVEMBER 10, 9A.M.-NOON

Public service announcements are just that, they proclaim or announce an event or cause that serves the public. When the St. Louis Public Library celebrated its centennial, I put the following message on the sign:

BIBLIOPHILES HAVE
100'S OF SMILES
THE LIBRARY IS 100!

When the library was promoting a registration drive for library cards, this sign made a great deal of sense:

THE CARD TO ACCESS
THE CARD OF SUCCESS
A LIBRARY CARD—CHECK IT OUT!

Our friends at the local branch of the library were thrilled that another non-profit would recognize and celebrate their birthday and promote a significant outreach project.

Every July 4th, our metro area celebrates by holding an event called "Fair St. Louis." In order to help remind people to "know when to say *when*" this sign called for everyone to think of the consequences when people drink too much alcohol:

BE FAIR TO YOURSELF
AND OTHERS
DON'T DRINK AND DRIVE!

Obviously, the key word to the phrase was "fair." The church sign can be a great help to other groups and agencies in your community.

We have donated the use of the sign (of course, I retain editorial rights) as an auction item for a Lutheran Social Service agency. Bidders have paid hundreds of dollars (given to the agency) to have an anniversary or birthday greeting placed on our sign. It is another way to have the sign enlighten and entertain.

Sometimes the church sign can speak for the community in a public way that no other entity can. For example, a local grocery store was closing its doors. Many elderly people in the community said, "I'm really going to miss Schnucks." So we lifted up that concern on the sign:

GOODBYE, SCHNUCKS
WE WILL MISS YOU!

I am very happy to say that after some time, the owners of

this particular chain of grocery stores put another store in our community. Of course, because we had said goodbye, we were very happy to say:

WELCOME BACK, SCHNUCKS!
WE'RE GLAD
WE'RE NEIGHBORS AGAIN!

When one of the largest fast food restaurants opened a store just a few blocks from church, we greeted them as well:

FOR SNACKS, TRY MACS.
FOR GRACE, TRY
THIS PLACE!

Our local neighborhood association sponsors an annual dining event called "The Tantalizing Taste of Tilles." (Tilles Park is our local park.) There are several fantastic dining places in our neighborhood that graciously offer their expertise and some of their products to help raise money for the community. This eye-catching sign supported the event:

LEADING US INTO TEMPTATION
THE TANTILIZING TASTES OF TILLES

When doing public service announcements it is important to think of the term "local" in three ways:

1. Local is the neighborhood, within a few blocks of the church building.
2. Local is city or countywide, events or causes that have a broad base of support.
3. Local means regional activities that are state or even bi-state in nature.

When the church does Public Service Announcements you are *announcing* to the *public* you are about service. Who could ask for anything more?

SIGNS I'D NEVER DO AGAIN
AND SIGNS I WISH I'D DO

BEARING FRUIT

The parable of the sower (Matthew 13) is an important one to remember. It is the calling of the believer in Jesus to sow the seed. All the rest comes from God. I am not a gardening expert, but I do know it is hard to just sow the seed. In my experience as a pastor, I want to be part of the team that brings in the harvest. I also want to make it rain and have the sun come out and dry up the cloudy, stormy days.

This section is about how the sign can bear fruit far beyond your imagination; how it can reach beyond the corners your church building, just like it has for us at the corner of Hampton and Pernod in south St. Louis, Missouri. It will also include some signs that might rate a lemon or two. Instead of being a sweet success they were sour experiences for people who pass by the church or for the church itself. However, you can learn from those as well what to do and what not to do again. For example, a medical study came out and stated the benefits of being "caffeine free." I wrote the following message to indicate that sermons at our church are so exciting caffeine is not needed to stay awake:

**THE SERMONS
HERE
ARE CAFFEINE FREE!**

Unfortunately, the message I was trying to share didn't *filter* through. People around the *grounds* of Gethsemane Lutheran Church simply didn't get it. And furthermore it became a *grind* to me trying to explain it. Another sign message that people simply didn't get was when I was trying to make a comment about palm reading or fortune telling. So I put this message on the sign:

**ANXIOUS ABOUT THE
FUTURE? PSALMS READ
EVERY SUNDAY.**

The collective response to the sign was "so what!" I thought the link between *palms* and *psalms* was humorous. But it didn't connect with where people were.

There is a popular St. Patrick's Day Parade in St. Louis. I was green with envy over all the public recognition of the event. So, I wanted to greet people with the message:

**TOP OF THE MORNING!
ENTERING NO BLARNEY ZONE.
GOD LOVES YOU!**

I thought *blarney* was a fairly common term, designating exaggerations or falsehoods. But several people called me up, having mis-read the sign and asked, "Why are you against Barney?" (You know, that purple dinosaur whose habitat is public television.) So, instead of getting any "green" in the offering plate, I received a little purple "bruise" because people perceived we were bashing Barney.

One year in order to advertise our ice cream social, we listed some of the food and events that would be offered. We were having pony rides, ice cream, games, and bratwurst. The Ice Cream Social is the concluding celebration for children who attended Vacation Bible School and their parents. So the sign read:

YOU SCREAM, WE ALL
SCREAM FOR ICE CREAM!
PONY RIDES, GAMES,
FUN, & BRATS!

Several mothers expressed their concern to me that I was calling their children "brats." I was shocked. It had nothing to do with children, but rather bratwurst, and I had simply run out of space and letters. My immediate response was, "Well, some of them are hot dogs, but I would never call them brats." However, I have not listed that particular abbreviation on the sign since then.

Another word that probably should not be placed on the sign is "assess." While it is important to analyze one's situation, my assessment is that people only read the first three letters of that particular word and begin wondering if the church is renting a donkey again for Palm Sunday. This underscores the "four eyes are better then two eyes" concept. Have someone else look at the proposed message before it is put on the sign. Ask people of different generations what specific words mean to them. And even when you have done all this and have corrected spelling and a good sign, it can still bring a negative comment.

During October 1990 there was a prominent person who "predicted" the possibility of an earthquake in this part of the country. The media immediately did stories about the need for earthquake insurance. Homeowners and business operators were reviewing their policies to determine the coverage in the event of an earthquake. So, I wrote:

NEED EARTHQUAKE
INSURANCE?
COME TO CHURCH

I remember receiving a couple of notes and several phone calls suggesting I was trying to scare people into church. While that was not my intention, it was perceived to be so. However, I think there may have been an element of insight to their concerns. One shouldn't joke about the potential of physical damage due to a natural event. It is much better to respond to a superstition regarding the number 13:

THE CURE OF TRISKIADEKAPHOBIA
IS THE TRIUNE GOD
3 IN ONE!

Triskiadekaphobia is the fear of the number 13. And it just seems right to invite people to know and believe that the Three In One, the One In Three is the answer to any fears they may have.

A local Lion's Club features a pancake breakfast. It has been my experience:

AS A CHRISTIAN,
IT IS BETTER TO BE FED
BY THE LIONS THAN TO THEM!

If the church sign is double-faced, you can send a message like this on one side and list the time and place and cost of the breakfast on the other side of the sign.

The St. Louis Symphony said farewell to a beloved conductor and selected Maestro Hans Vonk as the new conductor. There was some concern on the part of some music lovers regarding how the new conductor would be received. With a name like "Vonk," I decided to use a survey:

HONK!
IF YOU LOVE VONK!

Dozens of phone calls came into the office. Many people wanted to know what Vonk was. Yet many more people called (and honked) to say thank you for being hospitable to the new conductor and setting a nice tone in the community.

Whenever there is an event in which Roman numerals are used, (Super Bowls and Olympics, to name just a couple) I have listed the times of services in Roman numerals and even tried to do that with our phone number on one occasion. Warning: not even I or II people seem to get it. I was hoping someone would give me a "high V" but this practice has really been a zero!

One of the most popular signs that we have done referred to Jerry Seinfeld. The popularity of this particular sign reflected the popularity of the "Seinfeld" program that was going off the air:

SO LONG, JERRY,
FANS DON'T WORRY
THE BIBLE IS SIGN-FILLED!

The sign was quoted in the *St. Louis Post-Dispatch* and was mentioned on several radio programs.

My list of signs that "I wish to do" is pretty short. The reason for that is because if I wish to do them and they fit into the theme of enlightening and entertaining, they will be done. However, I would like to do more signs that deal with helping children and keeping them safe at home, in school, and in the community.

GUERILLA EVANGELISM

"You are the salt of the earth. But if salt loses its saltiness, how can it be made salty again?" (Matthew 5:13).

"You are the light of the world. A city on a hill cannot be hidden" (Matthew 5:14).

Our congregation practices what I refer to as "guerilla evangelism." If one were to describe churches in terms of grocery stores, then Gethsemane might be considered a mom-and-pop type operation. There are mega-churches, which are more along the lines of 24-hour grocery stores. For a decade now, I have strived to define Gethsemane's place in the community as a niche congregation. We are the neighborhood hardware store. Gethsemane fits the micro-church model in a world of international brewing. What we serve often has more taste, texture, and flavor than more popular brands (and we don't water anything down). We know we can't do it all. So what we do, we do very well.

We are progressive and traditional, socially aware, and yet non-partisan, hospitable, and tribal. Our place in the community is enhanced by excellent and relevant preaching (by the humble pastors), wonderful music, and a commitment to "Praising God, Preparing for Service, and Serving God, our members, and community." We have rehabbed houses for the homeless, imported coffee from

Panama and sold it under the name of our partner mission, and revitalized Vacation Bible School, which is perceived by many to be one of the best programs around town. It is central to our ministry that we conduct our selves as "salt and as light." These ingredients can enhance the flavor and bring preservation, can help germinate the process and bring illumination to the community. Note that sometimes the presence of these active agents is not even detected. Often the untrained eye doesn't even suspect there is anything at work. Furthermore, they follow a biblical principle based on service. As the salt flavors, as the light shines, each of them is decreased. Ultimately, the more they give, the sooner they will disappear from notice.

I have often shared with our leadership that our competition is not other Lutheran churches or even Protestant or Catholic congregations. I believe if prospective members visit our church, they will want to join. Or if a visit to our church helps them make a commitment to another part of Christ's kingdom, then we have been of service. It seems to me that some congregations are more interested in "building kingdoms" as opposed to "building the kingdom." Consequently, our competition (and I know church people don't often mention or say the "c" word) is places like the Missouri Botanical Gardens and the St. Louis Bread Company. Both of these places are wonderful (and I encourage people to visit them) Monday through Saturday and on Sundays after church. However, the two locales I have mentioned really know hospitality. Due to changes in the work force, coupled with mobility issues and changes in society in general, many people simply don't feel a part of something they can believe in. Consequently, projects and programs have been established at Gethsemane to help people find meaning in their daily life. It is very similar to what Jesus said to Simon and Andrew, "Come, follow Me" (Matthew 4:18).

Our church sign has been that salt for many people. During a very cold winter period, when local stores had run out of de-icer, we shared the message:

**LOVE IS THE
BEST DE-ICER!**

When a local business was being offered on the real estate market, we also listed our property:

THE CHURCH
NEEDS TO BE
SOULED!

Initially some people exclaimed, "Holy mackerel," and suspected there was something *fishy* going on. When questioned, I shared with them that I hoped it would help *net* some people.

I recently spoke at a gathering of business managers. Several of them told me that our church sign had kept them thinking about God during times when they weren't feeling "religious." One person remarked, "I was really feeling bad one day, and then I saw your sign:"

SPIRITS LOW?
COME IN FOR
A FAITH LIFT!

He said, "I started going to a church in my neighborhood the following Sunday and that's where I met my wife." I must tell you I had goosebumps as he related this story to me.

My dentist, who is a very gracious man and active in the ministry of the neighborhood Roman Catholic Church, always reminds me of a sign that made his day:

AVOID TRUTH DECAY
READ YOUR BIBLE!

I hope signs like that encourage people to *brush up* on the Scriptures. When they do, it is certain that any cavity they have will be filled.

As I have stated throughout this book, it is important to let your light shine. The illumination or insight that comes from the light of the world is so vitally needed in our communities. One particular summer it was very, very hot. People were very touchy and crabby. Our sign encouraged them to:

———

SMILE!
WE KNOW OF
HOTTER PLACES!

———

We believe it is "cool" to be a Christian. To literally:

———

TURN DOG DAYS
INTO GOD'S DAYS!

———

The church sign can be a major component in your congregation's evangelism program. It lets people know that you are thinking of them. And, most important, God loves them! Our congregation sponsors an ice cream social every year. The Sunday following that event we state:

———

NOTHING IS SWEETER
THAN ONE OF OUR
SUNDAYS!

———

Epilogue

NATE AND THE SIGN

A major insight came to me during the writing of this book—about my relationship to my 16 ½ year-old son, Nathan Theodore. Both of his names mean "Gift of God." He likes to refer to himself as "Gift of God Squared!"

Nathan Theodore is a very gifted young man. He has from time to time functioned as an apprentice "sign-changer." We have the usual parent-child, father-son, pastor-former confirmation student dynamics built into our relationship. There are times when we don't see eye to eye, although he now is tall enough to look me straight in the eye. Recently, I have found myself making statements to him that are more monological in nature than dialogical. In other words, I have said things and then made it quite clear that I consider the conversation closed. The discussion, as far as I am concerned, has ended. This hasn't strengthened our relationship but put stress and strain on it.

As I have been writing about how to make *Signs for These Times*, the thought came to me that I need to adopt a personal stance in line with the advice I have been giving. The goal and purpose of these signs is to enlighten and entertain. Being a teenager today is a "heavy" experience. I would add it's also a "heavy" experience to be a parent. The grace I've received by sharing these insights is that it is important to communicate during these times that Jesus is inviting all of us, "Come to Me, all you who are weary and burdened, and I will give you rest" (Matthew 11:28). It's a gift, a wondrous gift that I've received by giving to you through this book. I'm sure Nathan Theodore will appreciate receiving it too.

We are at our best when we send messages that encourage dialogue. It may come in the form of a question that needs clarification. One of my wife's coworkers always tells her that our church signs are a source of faith dialogue between her and her husband. Sometimes, she gets what the sign is all about when her husband doesn't get it at all. Conversely, on other occasions he gets it when she doesn't understand. The blessing in all of this is that they talk together about God and faith. Consequently, the goal of the sign to enlighten and entertain is being met.

As you go about the business of creating your own *Signs for These Times*, may you be blessed in your own faith walk and family communication as well. And remember that your enlightening and entertaining messages reach far beyond any place you can imagine. Pray that they are a blessing to all who read them.

Appendix A: "Merry Christmas" in Various Languages

Arabic	Eid Milad Said—Kol Aam Wa Antom Bee Kheir
Armenian	Shenoraavor Nor Dari yev Pari Gaghand
Brazilian	Feliz Natal e Feliz Ano Novo
Bulgarian	Tchestita Koleda; Tchesitito Rojdestvo Hristovo
Chinese (Mandarin)	Kung His Hsin Nien bing Chu Shen Tan
Chinese (Catonese)	Gun Tso Sun Tan'Gung Haw Sun
Croatian	Sretan Bozic
Czech	Prejeme Vam Vesele Vanoce a stastny Novy Rok
Danish	Glaedelig Jul; Godt Nyt Aar
Dutch	Vrolijk Kerstfeest en een Gelukkig Nieuwjaar!
Estonian	Roomsaid Joulu Puhi
Farsi Persian	Chrissmass Mobarak Saleh no mobarak
Finnish	Hauskaa joulua
French	Joyeux Noel
German	Froeliche Weihnachten
Greek	Kala Christouyenna!
Hebrew	Mo'adim Lesimkha. Chena tova
Hindi	Shub Naya Baras
Hungarian	Kellemas Karacsonyi unnepeket
Icelandic	Gledileg Jol

Indonesian	Selamat Hari Natal
Iraqi	Idah Saidan Wa Sanah Jadidah
Irish	Nodlaig mhaith chugnat
Italian	Buone Feste Natalizie
Japanese	Shinnen omedeto. Kurisumasu Omedeto
Korean	Sung Tan Chuk Ha
Latvian	Priecigus Ziemas Svetkus un Laimigu Jauno Gadu
Lithuanian	Linksmu Kaledu
Norwegian	God Jul Of Godt Nytt Aar
Polish	Wesolych Swiat Bozego Narodzenia
Portuguese	Boas Festas
Rumanian	Sarbatori vesele
Russian	Pozdrevlyayu s prazdnikom Rozhdest-va is Novim Godom
Serbian	Hristos se rodi
Slovakian	Sretan Bozic or Vesele vianoce
Slovak	Vesele Vianoce. A stastlivy Novy Rok
Spanish	Feliz Navidad
Swedish	God Jul and (Och) Ett Gott Nytt Ar
Turkish	Noeliniz Ve Yeni Yiliniz Kutlu Olsun
Ukrainian	Srozhdestvom Kristovym
Vietnamese	Chuc mung nam moic

APPENDIX B:
"THANK YOU" IN VARIOUS LANGUAGES

Arabic	shoukran
Czech	dekuji
Danish	tak
Dutch	dank
Esperanto	dankon
Finnish	kiitos
French	merci
German	danke
Greek	efcharisto
Hebrew	todah
Hungarian	koszonom
Indonesian	terima kasih
Italian	grazie
Japanese	kansha suru
Norwegian	takk
Portuguese	obrigado
Rumanian	multumiri
Russian	spasibo
Polish	dziekuje
Serbo-Croatian	hvala
Spanish	gracias
Swahili	asante
Swedish	tack
Turkish	tesekkur
Yiddish	dank

Appendix C:
"Peace" in Various Languages

Arabic	Sahlaahm
Burmese	Nyehn chahn yeh
Chinese	Ho P'ing
Filipino	Kapayapaan
French	Paix
German	Friede
Greek	Ihneenee
Hebrew	Shahlohm
Hindi	Shantee
Hungarian	Beke
Indonesian	Perdamaian
Irish	Siochain
Italian	Pace
Japanese	Haywah
Laotian	Santeefat
Latin	Pax
Persian	Sohl'h
Polish	Pokoj
Portuguese	Paz
Russian	Mir
Spanish	Paz
Swahili	Amani
Swedish	Fred
Thai	Santeepop
Vietnamese	Hoabinh

APPENDIX D: CHURCH SIGN TEMPLATE

Photocopy this page and use this template as you plan your signs. Don't forget to share your signs with several other people before you actually put them up! Then keep this in a file as a diary of signs you've used.

APPENDIX E: CHURCH YEAR CALENDAR 1998-2035

Year	Sundays after Epiphany	Ash Wednesday	Easter	Ascension	Pentecost	Sundays after Pentecost	First Advent Sunday
1998	7	Feb. 25	April 12	May 21	May 31	25	Nov. 29
1999	6	Feb. 17	April 4	May 13	May 23	26	Nov. 28
2000	9	March 8	April 23	June 1	June 11	24	Dec. 3
2001	8	Feb. 28	April 15	May 24	June 3	25	Dec. 2
2002	5	Feb. 13	March 31	May 9	May 19	27	Dec. 1
2003	8	March 5	April 20	May 29	June 8	24	Nov. 30
2004	7	Feb. 25	April 11	May 20	May 30	25	Nov. 28
2005	5	Feb. 9	March 27	May 5	May 15	27	Nov. 27
2006	8	March 1	April 16	May 25	June 4	25	Dec. 3
2007	7	Feb. 21	April 8	May 17	May 27	26	Dec. 2
2008	4	Feb. 6	March 23	May 1	May 11	28	Nov. 30
2009	7	Feb. 25	April 12	May 21	May 31	25	Nov. 29
2010	6	Feb. 17	April 4	May 13	May 23	26	Nov. 28
2011	9	March 9	April 24	June 2	June 12	23	Nov. 27
2012	7	Feb. 22	April 8	May 17	May 27	26	Dec. 2
2013	5	Feb. 13	March 31	May 9	May 19	27	Dec. 1
2014	8	March 5	April 20	May 29	June 8	24	Nov. 30
2015	6	Feb. 18	April 5	May 14	May 24	26	Nov. 29

2016	5	Feb. 10	March 27	May 5	May 15	27	Nov. 27
2017	8	March 1	April 16	May 25	June 4	25	Dec. 3
2018	6	Feb. 14	April 1	May 10	May 20	27	Dec. 2
2019	8	March 6	April 21	May 30	June 9	24	Dec. 1
2020	7	Feb. 26	April 12	May 21	May 31	25	Nov. 29
2021	6	Feb. 17	April 4	May 13	May 23	26	Nov. 28
2022	8	March 2	April 17	May 26	June 5	24	Nov. 27
2023	7	Feb. 22	April 9	May 18	May 28	26	Dec. 3
2024	6	Feb. 14	March 31	May 9	May 19	27	Dec. 1
2025	8	March 5	April 20	May 29	June 8	24	Nov. 30
2026	6	Feb. 18	April 5	May 14	May 24	26	Nov. 29
2027	5	Feb. 10	March 28	May 6	May 16	27	Nov. 28
2028	8	March 1	April 16	May 25	June 4	25	Dec. 3
2029	6	Feb. 14	April 1	May 10	May 20	27	Dec. 2
2030	8	March 6	April 21	May 30	June 9	24	Dec. 1
2031	7	Feb. 26	April 13	May 22	June 1	25	Nov. 30
2032	5	Feb. 11	March 28	May 6	May 16	27	Nov. 28
2033	8	March 2	April 17	May 26	June 5	24	Nov. 27
2034	7	Feb. 22	April 9	May 18	May 28	26	Dec. 3
2035	5	Feb. 7	March 25	May 3	May 13	28	Dec. 2

Appendix F: Sign Index

Homophones

Topic	Season/Time	Scripture
change	Lent	Joel 2:12–14

DO YOU WANT TO ALTER YOUR LIFE? WE STILL MAKE ALTAR CALLS!

change	Lent, any time	Matt. 5:23

LOOKING TO ALTER YOUR LIFE? COME TO THE ALTAR OF LIFE!

body of Christ	any time	1 Cor. 12:12

"NO ONE IS AN ISLE" FIND COMMUNITY IN ONE OF OUR AISLES!

Easter	Easter Sunday	John 20, 1 Cor. 15

MOURNING HAS BROKEN ON EASTER MORNING!

bombs	peace	Psalm 46:9

WE TRUST IN BALMS NOT BOMBS!

chants	music, chants	

SINCE THE 13TH CENTURY OUR CHANTS LEAVE NOTHING TO CHANCE

morals	mushroom hunting season	

WE DIG MORALS AND MORELS; WE HELP FAITH MUSHROOM AND GROW!

health, peace	any time	

CHURCH IS A HEALTHY PLACE; WE PASS THE PAX! NOT THE POX!

Any unseasonable weather, time
THE WEATHER SERVICE IS A NON-PROPHET ORGANIZATION—WE ARE NON-PROFIT!

heaven's gate, suicides
DON'T HALE BOPP HAIL CHRIST HE GIVES LIFE—DOESN'T TAKE IT
(contributed by Rev. Jeff Long)

shopping	November, December	

GOING CHOPIN? SPEND SOME MINUETS WITH GOD! COME BACH TO CHURCH!

prodigal son	any time	Luke 15

THE PRODIGAL SON WAS HAVING A BAD HEIR DAY!

spring time, bad air quality time		Luke 15

THE PRODIGAL SON DID NOT HAVE GOOD HEIR QUALITY!

Church Year

Topic	Season/Time	Scripture
Advent, holiday shopping	advent	

SHOP TILL YOU DROP? STAY TILL YOU PRAY!

Advent, Hanukkah, Kwanza	Advent	John 1:9

FOCUS ON THE CRECHE TO LIFT YOUR SPIRITS DUE TO THE HOLIDAY CRUSH

Advent, shopping	Advent, Christmas	

GOING CHOPIN? SPEND SOME MINUETS WITH GOD! COME BACH TO CHURCH!

Advent	Advent, Christmas	

JESUS IS THE REASON FOR THE SEASON!

Advent	Advent	

ADVENT—THE PAUSE THAT REFRESHES!

Advent	Advent	Mark 1

JOIN US FOR THE READING OF THE AX OF JOHN THE BAPTIST STUDY THE ACTS AND ROOTS OF CHRISTMAS

Advent, aria	Advent, Christmas	

OUR AREA HAS LOTS OF ARIAS COME SING WITH US!

Christmas carols	Advent, Christmas	Psalm 23

KIDS—LEARN CAROLS NOW! YOU HAVE MORE RAM WHEN YOU'RE A LITTLE LAMB!

Christmas, welcome	Christmas	

WELCOME ANGELS, SHEPHERDS, WISEONES, EVEN GRINCHES & SCROOGES!

Christmas manger	Christmas	Luke 2

THE BABY IN THE MANGER SPELLS OUT GOD'S TERMS OF ENDEARMENT

Christmas manger	Christmas	John 1

"GOD IS WATCHING US" FROM THE MANGER!

Christmas values	Christmas	Matthew 1–3

HOLY FAMILY VALUES ACCEPTANCE, PONDERING, & BEING STILL

Christmas magi	Christmas, Epiphany	Matthew 2

THE MAGI—1ST CENTURY SPICEBOYS! THEY KNEW BABY AS REASON FOR SEASON

New Year, Epiphany	Epiphany	

FOR A HAPPY NEW YEAR, COME IN & LEARN HOW TO BE A HAPPY NEW YOU!

Epiphany, Star Trek	Epiphany	Matthew 2

EPIPHANY AN ENTERPRISING STAR TREK!

Topic	Season/Time	Scripture

New Years re-solutions   New Years   John 14:6
IN ORDER TO RE-SOLVE PROBLEMS GOD IS THE ANSWER & AUTHOR OF
NEW YEAR'S RESOLUTIONS

Epiphany, magi   Epiphany   Matthew 2
WISE WOMEN, WISE MEN, WISE BOYS, & WISE GIRLS STILL SEEK HIM! FOLLOW
THE STAR!

Ground hog, light   Ground Hog's Day   John 8:12
SEEING SHADOWS? COME TO THE LIGHT!

Ground hog, shadows   Ground Hog's Day
WHETHER OR NOT IT IS SHADOWS CHURCH CAN HELP YOU WEATHER THE
STORMS OF LIFE!

Shadows   Ground Hog's Day
WE BELIEVE THAT SOMEONE ELSE KNOWS MORE THAN THE SHADOW
KNOWS

Lent, ashes   Lent   Psalm 103:14
ASHES, ASHES WE ALL FALL DOWN!

Lent, ashes   Lent, Holy Week
MARCH MADNESS FROM ASHES TO LILIES

Lent, repent   Lent   Joel 2:12–14
LENT U-TURNS PERMITTED AND ENCOURAGED

Lent, discipline   Lent, Spring Training
LENT IS SPRING TRAINING FOR CHRISTIANS

Lent, potholes   Lent
LENT A TIME TO FILL IN THE POTHOLES OF LIFE

Lent   Lenten classes or services
LENT SPIRITUAL "TOOL TIME" FOR "HOME IMPROVEMENT"

Lent, taxes   Lent, tax-prep time
WE OFFER COUNSEL SO YOU ARE NOT AUDITED ON YOUR FINAL RETURN!

Lent, tax deduct   Lent, tax time   Psalm 51
DEDUCT SIN EXEMPTIONS FROM YOUR SPIRITUAL 1040 FORM

Lent, tax refund   Lent, tax time
TO MAKE TAX TIME LESS TAXING REFUNDS ACCEPTED HERE!

Lent   Lent   Acts 1:11
LENT IS TIME TO CALCULATE THE FINAL RETURN OF JESUS!

Topic	Season/Time	Scripture

Holy Week, lion/lamb	Holy Week, march madness	Mark 11
MARCH MADNESS IN LIKE A LION! OUT LIKE A LAMB!		
Holy Week, lion/lamb	palm/passion Sunday	Mark 11
WE DON'T READ PALMS WE WAVE THEM HOSANNA!		
Lent, Good Friday	Good Friday	Mark 15
THE "FOOL ON THE HILL" IS THERE FOR YOU & ME!"		
Lent, cross	Good Friday	Mark 15
PASSENGERS AND CREW THE CAPTAIN STATES " PREPARE FOR CROSS CHECK"		
Lent, TGIF	Good Friday	Mark 15
THANK GOD IT'S GOOD FRIDAY!		
Easter, open on Sunday	Easter	Luke 24
WE'RE OPEN ON SUNDAY BECAUSE THE TOMB WAS OPEN ON SUNDAY!		
Easter, eggs	Easter	1 Corinthians 15
EASTER MORE THAN SOMETHING TO DYE FOR!		
Easter, spice girls	Easter	Mark 16
JOANNA, MARY, & MARY MAGDALENE THE ORIGINAL SPICE GIRLS		
Easter, eggs	Easter time	
SCRAMBLING FOR FUN? TILLES PARK EGGHUNT 11 A.M–1 P.M. ON EASTER SATURDAY		
Easter, movies	Easter, time change weekend	Mark 16
SPRING FORWARD DEAD MAN RISEN! ALLELUIA!		
Easter, grief	Easter	1 Corinthians 15
MOURNING HAS BROKEN ON EASTER MORNING!		
Easter, new life	Easter	
BREAK OUT OF YOUR SHELL CELEBRATE NEW LIFE!		
Easter, doubt, hope	the Sunday after Easter	John 20
DOUBTERS WELCOME!		
Easter, sheep	Sundays after Easter	Psalm 23, John 10
CAN'T SLEEP? COUNTING SHEEP? TALK TO THE SHEPHERD!		
Ascension Day	Ascension Day	Acts 1
ASCENSION DAY IT'S AN UP THING!		
Ascension Day, up & down	Ascension Day	Acts 1:11
ASCENSION DAY—WHAT GOES UP WILL COM DOWN! IT'S GRACE NOT GRAVITY!		

Topic	Season/Time	Scripture

Pentecost — Pentecost — Acts 2
UNDER THE SAME MANAGEMENT SINCE PENTECOST 33 A.D.

Pentecost, air spirit — Pentecost — Acts 2
OUT OF BREATH? GET PUMPED UP WITH SPIRITUAL CPR—FREE AIR!

Pentecost, air pressure — Pentecost — Luke 15, Psalm 51
THE PRODIGAL SON HAD LOW HEIR PRESSURE FILL UP WITH THE RIGHT SPIRIT!

Trinity Sunday, Friday the 13th — Friday the 13th, Trinity
THE CURE OF TRISKAIDEKAPHOBIA IS THE TRIUNE GOD 3 IN 1!

Memorial Day
REMEMBER! THE WOMEN AND MEN WHO SERVED AND SERVE SO WE CAN HAVE FREEDOM!

4th of July, blast — 4th of July
LITANY FIREWORKS? SPARK YOUR FAITH & HAVE A BLAST IN LIFE!

Reformation Day — Halloween, Ref. Sunday — John 3:16
IT'S A TREAT NOT A TRICK GOD LOVES YOU!

All Saints — All Saints Sunday
FOR ALL YOU DO THIS ONE'S FOR YOU! ALL SAINTS' SUNDAY!

All Saints — All Saints Sunday
BELIEVE IT OR NOT SAINTS (R) US!

Thanksgiving, turkeys — Thanksgiving — Philippians 1:3
THANKSGIVING—ONLY TURKEYS DON'T GIVE THANKS!

Thanksgiving — Thanksgiving
THANKSGIVING HAPPENS! GRACIAS, DANKE, MERCI!

Movies—Gospel According to Hollywood

Topic	Season/Time	Scripture

forgiveness — Matthew 6
A DECENT PROPOSAL FORGIVE AS WE HAVE BEEN FORGIVEN

Bible — Oscar or Academy Awards
MOVIES—REEL LIFE THE BIBLE—REAL LIFE STILL THE BEST SELLER

Bible — 2 Timothy 3:16, John 14
THE BIBLE TEACHES SENSE AND SENSIBILITY FOR BRAVE HEARTS

Bible — John 8
TIRED OF PULP FICTION? BE ENERGIZED BY THE WORLD OF TRUTH

Topic	Season/Time	Scripture

movies   John 3:16
UNFORGIVEN? CRYING GAME? JESUS DIED FOR YOU!

manger   Advent/Christmas   Luke 2
THE BABY IN THE MANGER SPELLS OUT GOD'S TERMS OF ENDEARMENT

Flintstones   Psalm 92:15
A BEDROCK FAITH YABBA-DABBA-DO GOD LOVES YOU!

movies   Acts 2:42
HOME ALONE 2? COME TOGETHER AT CHURCH!

movies
CHURCH IS LIKE A BOX OF CHOCOLATES …

hope   Hebrews 6:19
DO YOU HAVE A TITANIC SINKING FEELING? HOPE WILL FLOAT YOUR BOAT!

new life   Easter, time change   1 Corinthians 15
SPRING FORWARD DEAD MAN RISEN ALLELUIA!

teachings   1 Corinthians 13
WE TEACH "GOOD WILL HUNTING" & THIS IS NOT "AS GOOD AS IT GETS"

Bible   2 Timothy 3:16
THE BIBLE WRITTEN "ON THE WINGS OF A DOVE" & QUOTES "THE APOSTLE"

Bible   2 Timothy 3:16
THE BIBLE WHEN READ AND APPLIED MAKES DEEP IMPACT!

goodness   Galatians 5:22–24
GOOD WILL PRAYING FOR ALL PEOPLE!

space
LOST IN SPACE? THE BIBLE WILL HELP YOU MAKE CONTACT!

Pentecost   Pentecost   Acts 2
PENTECOST—THE ORIGINAL MISSION POSSIBLE

Revelation   Movies about the end of time   Revelation
HAVE YOU SEE ARMAGEDDON? COME HEAR THE REST OF THE STORY!

Letterman
TRY THE LETTERMAN OF THE BIBLE—ST. PAUL!

Worry, confession   Matthew 6:25
DOWNLOAD YOUR WORRIES GET ON-LINE WITH GOD!

Trends

software upgrades   new software, products
OUR WINDOWS WILL HELP YOU UPGRADE!

bungee cords   Hebrews 11
NO BUNGEE CORDS BUT WE ENCOURAGE LEAPS OF FAITH!

trends   new soda marketing campaign   1 Corinthians 13
THE REAL SECRET INGREDIENT IS LOVE UH HUH!

trends   new clear soda mkt. campaign   1 Corinthians 13:12
CRYSTAL CLEAR GOSPEL IS HERE!

mergers   merger mania   John 17
PRAYER IS MERGER TALK WITH GOD & YOU BUILD A BOND; INVEST NOW!

gambling   new casinos in region   Psalm 105:1
GAMBLING WHEEL OF MIS-FORTUNE SOLVE THE PUZZLE WITH PRAYER!

gambling   out of luck   Matthew 28:20
WE DON'T HAVE POWERBALL TICKETS BECAUSE WITH GOD YOU'RE A NAME, NOT A NUMBER! YOU CAN BET YOUR LIFE!

rock concert   Psalm 19:14
ROLLING STONES "BRIDGES TO BABYLON" GOD-SOLID ROCK "A BRIDGE TO PROMISED LAND"

live TV   Acts 10:43
IF YOU HAVE "ER"-RED, EXPERIENCE FORGIVENESS LIVE ON SUNDAYS!

Seinfeld show   farewell seinfeld show, re-runs   John 21:25
SO LONG, JERRY FANS DON'T WORRY THE BIBLE IS SIGN-FILLED!

cold season   frigid temperatures   1 Corinthians 13
LOVE IS THE BEST DE-ICER!

soul   for sale signs on local businesses
THE CHURCH NEEDS TO BE SOULED!

bank sold   any time a bank is sold or merged
CHURCH—WE HAVE A TRUST DEPARTMENT YOU CAN BANK ON!

G. Keillor concert   G. Keillor comes to town
WE ARE THE LUTHERANS GARRISON KEILLOR TALKS ABOUT!

cloning   cloning research
THE SHEEP WE'D CLONE ARE ALTOS, TENORS, AND TITHERS!

Topic	*Season/Time*	*Scripture*

public TV   3 tenors concert
WE HAVE "3 TENORS" BUT WE'D LIKE MORE! COME SING WITH US!

bank   local bank spokesperson fired
WE WANT TO HELP SAVE THE BOATMAN'S BUY & EVERYONE ELSE, TOO!

heat-wave   hot, hot, steamy temps
SMILE! WE KNOW OF HOTTER PLACES!

super-sized   fast-food marketing campaign
READ THE BIBLE & GET YOUR FAITH SUPER-SIZED—FOR FREE!

Mars trip   exploration of Mars   Galatians 3:28
MARTIANS WELCOME! WE HAVE SPACE FOR EVERYONE!

UFOs   UFO sightings, movies
WE BELIEVE IN UFO'S—UNITY, FORGIVENESS, & OUTREACH!

cw song   popular country song   Psalm 51
ACHY BREAKY HEARTS ARE HEALED AT CHURCH!

deaths of popular people   Mother Teresa & Princess Di   John 8
A CANDLE IN THE WIND A LIGHT IN THE DARK REFLECT LOVE FROM
ABOVE!

reading of palms   Colossians 3:16
ANXIOUS ABOUT THE FUTURE? PSALM READ EVERY SUNDAY!

caffeine free
THE SERMONS HERE ARE CAFFEINE FREE!

falling comets
IF THE CONCERN IS SAFETY WE ARE COMET DEBRIS FREE!

MTV unplug   unplugged concerts
UNPLUGGED? PLUG IN & GET CURRENT WITH GOD!

Zima beer   marketing campaign for beer with "Z"
THINK CHURCH IS ZZZ? ZOMETHING ZPECIAL EACH ZUNDAY!

"hair days"   Luke 15
THE PRODIGAL SON WAS HAVING A BAD HEIR DAY!

karaoke
BETTER THAN KARAOKE COME SING WITH US!

St. Patrick's Day
TOP OF THE MORNING! ENTERING NO BLARNEY ZONE GOD LOVES YOU!

Sports

Topic	Season/Time	Scripture

football · Super Bowl
OUR SUPER SUNDAY IS COMMERCIAL FREE! HEAR THE WORD FROM OUR SPONSOR!

football · Super Bowl
SUPER SUNDAY'S SERMON IS A $37.5 MILLION BARGAIN 12.5 MIN X 3 MILLION A MINUTE

football · Super Bowl
EVERY SUNDAY HERE IS SUPER SUNDAY!

soccer · World Cup
OUR GOAL ON SUNDAYS IS TO CELEBRATE THE CUP FOR THE WORLD!

general · season tickets sales
THE CHURCH IS A PSL PEOPLE-SERVING-LOVING!

football · receiving an NFL franchise
TOUCHDOWN! WELL DONE! FANS INC!

general · ticket sales
OUR LUXURY BOXES ARE FREE!

hockey · playoffs
HOCKEY PLAYOFF SPECIAL DELIVERY FREE PRAY PER PEW!

hockey
FEEL LIKE YOU'RE IN A PENALTY BOX? FEEL FREEDOM IN CHURCH!

race cars · Memorial Day or any race time
ON THE RACE TRACK OF LIFE MAKE PIT STOPS—PRAY, INSPIRE, TOUCH!

golf · PGA tournament · 1 Thessalonians 5:16–17
PGA—PRAISE GOD ALWAYS

baseball
ROSEANNE BARR DOESN'T SING HERE BUT YOU CAN!

football · any visiting team
49ERS FANS WELCOME!

Olympics
IN LIFE'S OLYMPICS GO FOR THE GOLD IN KINDNESS

baseball · Opening day or World series · Genesis 1:1
BASEBALL IS BIBLICAL—IN THE "BIG INNING"

Topic	Season/Time	Scripture
tennis		Genesis 41

TENNIS IS BIBLICAL—JOSEPH SERVED IN PHARAOH'S COURTS!

baseball	World Series	

ENJOY THE WORLD SERIES! COME HERE AND ENJOY THE WORD SERIOUS!

golf		

GOLFERS WELCOME! WE OFTEN TALK ABOUT EAGLES AND BIRDIES
& BEING WHOLE IN ONE!

basketball	Spring, Holy Week	Mark 11

MARCH MADNESS FROM ASHES TO LILIES

baseball	spring training, Lent	

LENT IS SPRING TRAINING FOR CHRISTIANS

Politics

Topics	Season/Time	Scripture
debates	elections	

THERE IS NO DEBATE! GOD LOVES YOU!

voting	elections	

BAD PEOPLE ARE ELECTED BY GOOD PEOPLE WHO DON'T VOTE!

voting	elections	

VOTE—VOICE OF THE ELECTORATE JUST DO IT!

voting	elections	

"VOTE" IS A FOUR LETTER WORD—HANDLE WITH PRAYER!

free speech	supreme court ruling	

AREN'T YOU GLAD THIS SIGN ISN'T IN LADUE? WE ARE!

free speech	supreme court ruling	

PRAYERS ARE STILL LEGAL HERE!

Time

Topic	Season/Time	Scripture
time	spring or early summer	Exodus 20:8–11

ARE YOU WEAKENED AFTER THE WEEKEND? GET RE-CHARGED WITH GOD!

spice	Fall, Thanksgiving	

WANT SPICE IN YOUR LIFE? SPEND THYME AT CHURCH & BECOME SAGE!
ROSEMARY DID!

Topic	Season/Time	Scripture

time   spring time change
DID YOU LOSE AN HOUR? SO DID PASTOR—SHORT SERMON ON SUNDAY!

time   spring time change
LOSE AN HOUR? FIND THE TIME OF YOUR LIFE AT CHURCH!

time   fall time change
USE YOUR EXTRA HOUR TO MAKE ST. LOUIS BETTER!

time   any time   2 Peter 3:8
PASTOR'S SERMONS ARE SHORT BUT "SHORT" IS RELATIVE WHEN YOU ARE TALKING ABOUT ETERNITY!

worship   summer
NOTHING IS SWEETER THAN ONE OF OUR SUNDAYS!

Potpourri

Topic	Season/Time	Scripture

final exams   graduation
WE WILL HELP YOU STUDY FOR YOUR FINAL EXAM!

deer hunting mission   deer season
OUR OFFERINGS SUPPORT MISSIONS AROUND THE WORLD, SO THE BUCK DOESN'T STOP HERE!

Lions Club   Lions Club pancake luncheon (fall)
AS A CHRISTIAN IT IS BETTER TO BE FED BY THE LIONS THAN TO THEM!

Moses   any time   Exodus 3
THE FIRST ROAD SIGN WAS THE BURNING BUSH. WHAT'S HOT IN YOUR LIFE?

Public Service Announcements

Topic	Season/Time

time   fall time change
USE YOUR EXTRA HOUR TO HELP MAKE ST. LOUIS BETTER!

+ & - people   blood drive
WE WANT NEGATIVE & POSITIVE PEOPLE GLD & SJA BLOOD DRIVE SAT. 9–12

volunteers   blood drive
WE NEED YOUR TYPE! BLOOD DRIVE SAT. 9–12

Topic	Season/Time	Scripture

library card   library month
THE CARD TO ACCESS THE CAR OF SUCCESS A LIBRARY CARD—CHECK IT
OUT!

library   anniversary of library
BIBLIOPHILES HAVE 100S OF SMILES THE LIBRARY IS 100!

blues   jazz concert
GOT THE BLUES? FREE JAZZ CONCERT! 7 P.M. SATURDAY

fair   4th of July
BE FAIR TO YOURSELF AND OTHERS DON'T DRINK & DRIVE

fair   4th of July
CELEBRATE THE 4TH SO YOU CAN ENJOY THE 5TH DON'T DRINK AND
DRIVE!

store closing
GOODBYE SCHNUCKS WE WILL MISS YOU!

store re-opening
WELCOME BACK, SCHNUCKS WE'RE GLAD WE'RE NEIGHBORS AGAIN!

McDonald's   new restaurant in area
FOR SNACKS TRY MACS, FOR GRACE TRY THIS PLACE

temptation   neighborhood food festival
"LEADING US INTO TEMPTATION" THE TANTALIZING TASTE OF TILLES

dine out for life   AIDS research fundraiser
DINE OUT FOR LIFE DEC. 2 TUESDAY SHARING—HELPING

flood relief   sandbagging
SANDBAGGING LOVE IN ACTION!

"Kiss Me Kate" play   Note: the humor here involves the fact that
Luther's wife was Katie. A local Roman Catholic church was presenting the play
"Kiss Me Kate," so our sign read:
MARTIN LUTHER SAID, "KISS ME KATE" SO DOES ST. GABRIEL'S

honk   new symphony director
MUSIC APPRECIATION HONK! IF YOU LOVE VONK!

Muny Opera presents JC Superstar
AFTER THE PLAY JC SUPERSTAR COME & PRAY TO JC SUPERSTAR

Bach   Bachfest
THE BACH STOPS HERE—JS THAT IS! BACHFEST

Topic	*Season/Time*	*Scripture*

angels   Art exhibit of "Angels from Vatican"
HEAVENLY ADVICE–WING ON OVER TO THE ART MUSEUM AND SAY, "HALO!"

interpreter for deaf
THE CHURCH WITH THE SIGN HAS A SIGN FOR THE DEAF SUNDAYS 11 A.M.

vote   election time, Veterans Day
VOTING IS FREE THANK THE VETERANS YOU SEE!

holidays   any time people come home
REMEMBER! CHURCH IS HOME FOR THE HOLIDAYS!

Muny Opera anniversary
HAPPY 75TH ANNIVERSARY FOR THE MUNY!

fun run   any fun run
5K RUN FOR THE HILLS A BENEFIT FOR FRANCIS PARK SAT SEPT 17

anniversary   centennial celebration
100TH ANNIVERSARY OVER 10,000 SERMONS SERVED! FREE COFFEE!

time change   fall time change
TREAT YOURSELF TO AN EXTRA HOUR OF CHURCH THIS WEEKEND!

love   Valentine's Day
IT IS GOOD TO SAY "I LOVE YOU" JUST ABOUT ANY DAY!

death of P.M. Rabin   Recognition of death of world leader
BLESSED ARE THE PEACEMAKERS PRIME MINISTER RABIN

car wash   police explorer's car wash
GRIME DOESN'T PAY POLICE EXPLORER CAR WASH SUNDAY

peace prayer   times of conflict in community or world
PRAY FOR PEACE, PAX, PAZ, SHALOM!

low mood   times of the year when people need a "boost"
SPIRITS LOW? COME IN FOR A FAITH LIFT!

Bible reading   during a time when there is a focus on dental hygiene
                                                            John 8:36
AVOID TRUTH DECAY BRUSH UP ON YOUR BIBLE!

dog days   hot, hot summer time
TURN DOG DAYS INTO GOD'S DAYS!

garage, rummage sales   neighborhood/community sales
SAY "YES" TO NAYBORHOOD GARAGE SALES!